DK EYEWITNESS

T0276883

TOP 10
FLORENCE
AND TUSCANY

Top 10 Florence and Tuscany Highlights

The Top 10 of Everything

CONTENTS

Florence and Tuscany Area by Area

Streetsmart

The rapid rate at which the world is changing is constantly keeping the DK Eyewitness team on our toes. While we've worked hard to ensure that this edition of Florence and Tuscany is accurate and up-to-date, we know that opening hours alter, standards shift, prices fluctuate, places close and new ones pop up in their stead. So, if you notice we've got something wrong or left something out, we want to hear about it. Please get in touch at **travelguides@dk.com**

Welcome to
Florence
and Tuscany

Florence's Piazza della Signoria as the morning sun hits the Palazzo Vecchio. A distant ridge dotted with cypress trees. A sizzling Chianina steak fresh from the flame grill. It is for these moments, and many more, that travellers have been visiting Tuscany for centuries. With DK Eyewitness Top 10 Florence and Tuscany, it's yours to explore.

At the region's heart sits **Florence**, city of the Renaissance and buzzing home to modern style icons like Gucci and Ferragamo. Here you'll discover many of the world's great paintings and sculptures, including those in the masterpiece-packed **Uffizi**, **Accademia** and **Pitti Palace**. In the shadow of Brunelleschi's iconic **Duomo** dome are cobblestoned streets upon which Dante and Michelangelo walked.

Beyond the Florence city limits are hill towns like **San Gimignano**, with stone towers and twisting alleys barely changed since the 1300s. **Siena** is a treasure-trove of paintings left by the trailblazers of Western art, while **Pisa** has the world's most photographed bit of botched architecture in one of Italy's most photogenic piazzas. The sublime landscapes of the **Chianti** and **Val d'Orcia** regions change dramatically with the passing of the seasons.

Whether you're visiting for a weekend or a week, our Top 10 guide brings together the best of everything that Florence and Tuscany have to offer, from the hip, contemporary restaurants of **San Frediano** in Florence to the winelands of **Montepulciano** and **Montalcino**. The guide has useful tips throughout, from seeking out what's free to how to get off the beaten track, plus ten easy-to-follow itineraries designed to tie together a clutch of sights in a short space of time. Add inspiring photography and detailed maps, and you've got the essential pocket-sized travel companion. **Enjoy the book, and enjoy Florence and Tuscany.**

Clockwise from top: **Sorano, Pisa's Leaning Tower, the Tuscan countryside, Florence's Pitti Palace, Michelangelo's** *David***, Viareggio's Carnevale, Montepulciano's Palazzo Bucelli**

Exploring Florence and Tuscany

With its world-famous art cities, exquisite medieval hill towns and iconic vine- and olive-clad hills, Tuscany has so much to see that it can be difficult to decide where to start. These itineraries are designed to make planning your trip easy, concentrating on the places that no one should miss.

Key

— Two-day itinerary
— Seven-day itinerary

Florence's Ponte Vecchio still has shops on it, as was common in the Middle Ages.

Two Days in Florence

Day ❶

MORNING

Begin with the splendid **Duomo Group** (see pp16–17). Climb to the top of the Campanile then admire the Gothic Baptistry. Walk to **Piazza della Signoria** (see p83), which is overlooked by **Palazzo Vecchio** (see p83), then cross the Arno via the medieval **Ponte Vecchio** (see p82) with its minuscule jewellery shops.

AFTERNOON

Visit the **Pitti Palace** (see pp18–21) for Raphael's *La Velata* then stroll around the Boboli Gardens. End the day at the **Uffizi** (see pp12–15), being sure to admire Botticelli's *La Primavera* and *Birth of Venus*.

Day ❷

MORNING

Head to **Santa Croce** (see p82), where the Cappella Pazzi is an icon of Renaissance architecture, then move on to **Il Bargello** (see p82), which houses sculptures including *Flying Mercury* by Giambologna. Devote the rest of the morning to Fra Angelico's frescoes at **San Marco** (see p82).

AFTERNOON

Pay homage to Michelangelo's *David* at the **Galleria dell'Accademia** (see p81). Afterwards, look at scenes from the New Testament by Ghirlandaio in the church of **Santa Maria Novella** (see p52). Take bus 12 (or a short walk) from the train station to **San Miniato al Monte** (see p53), for splendid views and a marble medieval horoscope.

The beautiful Tuscan countryside is dotted with iconic cypress trees.

Seven Days in Tuscany

Days ❶ and ❷
Follow the two-day Florence itinerary.

Day ❸
Arrive in **Pisa** *(see pp26–9)* and make a beeline for the Piazza del Duomo, dominated by the Leaning Tower. Next, visit the market on arcaded Piazza Vettovaglie and then stroll along the languid Arno before driving to **Lucca** *(see pp46–7)*.

Day ❹
Begin at Lucca's Duomo, housing the *Volto Santo*. Next, walk around the town's ramparts before heading to the Piazza del Mercato, which still retains the form of the Roman amphi-theatre that preceded it. Then drive south to **San Gimignano** *(see pp24–5)*, for its medieval towers and formidably crenellated private and civic buildings. Visit the Collegiata with its 14th-century fres-coes by Bartolo di Fredi. Pick up an ice cream at Piazza della Cisterna's Gelateria "di Piazza" (Gelateria Dondoli).

Day ❺
Tour the **Chianti Classico** wine region *(see pp38–41)*, stopping for tasters along the way. From Panzano a minor road leads to the picturesque wine hamlet of Volpaia, close to Radda in Chianti. Afterwards, head through the scenic Tuscan countryside to **Siena** *(see pp30–37)*.

Day ❻
Explore Piazza del Campo and visit the medieval art collection of the Palazzo Pubblico. Climb the Torre del Mangia, before heading to the striped Duomo. In the evening, drive to **Cortona** *(see pp42–5)*.

Day ❼
Spend the morning in **Cortona** *(see pp42–5)*, with its Etruscan museum and tombs and medieval alleyways. Be sure to visit the Museo Diocesano for Fra Angelico's *Annunciation* before driving back to Florence.

San Gimignano, with its imposing medieval towers, is one of Tuscany's most evocative hill towns.

Top 10 Florence and Tuscany Highlights

Marble façade and campanile of
the Duomo in Florence

🔟 Florence and Tuscany Highlights

Limiting the choice of prime sights to ten is not an easy task in a land as rich and varied as Tuscany. Its storybook landscape is home to medieval hill towns, fabled wines and an unrivalled collection of Renaissance artistic masterpieces. Here are the best of the best.

The Uffizi, Florence ①

A veritable who's who of the greatest Renaissance masters is installed in the former *uffizi* ("offices") of Florence's ruling Medici family *(see pp12–15)*.

② The Duomo Group, Florence

Brunelleschi's noble dome, Giotto's slender bell tower, Ghiberti's robust gates, Michelangelo's tortured *Pietà* and two panoramic terraces, all wrapped in red, white and green marble, are a magnificent sight *(see pp16–17)*.

Pitti Palace, Florence ③

This massive Medici palace has a painting collection to rival the Uffizi, with porcelain, silver, carriages and modern art on display, as well as formal gardens *(see pp18–21)*.

San Gimignano ④

A medieval fairy-tale town with stone towers and frescoed churches, surrounded by patchwork fields and terraced vineyards *(see pp24–5)*.

5 Piazza del Duomo, Pisa

This iconic grassy piazza is studded with masterpieces of Romanesque architecture: the Baptistry and Duomo containing Gothic pulpits by the Pisanos and, of course, that famous leaning bell tower *(see pp26–9)*.

6 Siena's Duomo

A striped giant of a cathedral, the Duomo is stuffed with carvings, frescoes, Michelangelo's sculptures and Bernini's chapel *(see pp30–33)*.

7 Siena's Campo and Palazzo Pubblico

This brick square is Siena's living room, its graceful Palazzo Pubblico has a museum celebrating the maestros of Gothic art *(see pp34–7)*.

8 Chianti

The ultimate Tuscan idyll, this is a landscape of steeply rolling hills clad in rows of grapevines, topped by castles and dotted with countryside *trattorie* serving up Italy's most famous wine *(see pp38–41)*.

9 Cortona

This is Tuscany in miniature: medieval atmosphere, great art, handcrafted ceramics, sweeping views and fine wines *(see pp42–5)*.

10 Lucca

Medieval towers and 16th-century ramparts have been domesticated as small parks in this elegant city of Romanesque façades and opera *(see pp46–7)*.

🔟 ⭐ The Uffizi, Florence

This museum is the ultimate Renaissance primer, from Giotto, Botticelli, Leonardo da Vinci and Michelangelo to Raphael, Titian, Caravaggio and Gentileschi. This historic progression is only fitting, as the building, originally the *uffizi* ("offices") of the ruling Medici family, was designed by Giorgio Vasari, who wrote the world's first art history text. Some 1,700 works are on display, with another 1,400 in storage. These galleries shelter an abundance of masterpieces that demand a visit of at least three or four hours.

5 Madonna of the Magnificat

Botticelli explores the idea of beauty in this work of art. Round paintings, such as this *tondo*, were usually displayed in secular settings and not in churches. The sophisticated gestures and fine fabrics portrayed in the painting make the scene look more courtly than traditionally religious.

6 Madonna of the Goldfinch

Painted during Raphael's Florentine period (c.1504–8), *Madonna of the Goldfinch* **(below)** contains symbolic elements that foreshadow the sacrifice of Christ, evoked by the innocently fragile goldfinch.

1 Birth of Venus

Botticelli's Venus on a shell (c.1484–6) is the ultimate Renaissance beauty **(above)**. While the pose is classical, the face is said to be Simonetta Vespucci's, the girlfriend of Piero de' Medici, and cousin to the explorer Amerigo Vespucci.

2 Madonna with Child and Two Angels

This painting (c.1565) by Filippo Lippi is one of the most admired of the Renaissance. Its composition would become a model for many painters, such as Botticelli. The landscape is inspired by Flemish paintings.

3 Tondo Doni

The *Tondo Doni* or *Holy Family* is a rare panel painting (1504) by Michelangelo. It owes much to Signorelli, but its saturated colours, twisting figures and lounging nudes predict Mannerism.

4 La Primavera

Botticelli's companion work to his *Birth of Venus*, *La Primavera* (1478) is populated by goddesses and over 500 species of plants. The painting's exact meaning is not known but it may be a Neoplatonic allegory of spring based around a poem by Poliziano.

7 Federico da Montefeltro and Battista Sforza

Piero della Francesca's intense, psychological style unflinchingly depicts his patrons, the Duke **(left)** and Duchess of Urbino, warts and all.

MUSEUM GUIDE

Coming from the Piazza della Signoria, enter on the left (east) side of the U-shaped loggia; one entrance is for reserved tickets and Firenze Card holders, the other for walk-ins. The top-floor galleries line a long corridor. Rooms 2–22 are in the east wing, 24 is in the south corridor, and 24–42 are in the west. The newer Sale Blu, Rosse and Gialle (Blue, Red and Yellow Rooms) downstairs double back towards the shop next to the entrance/exit.

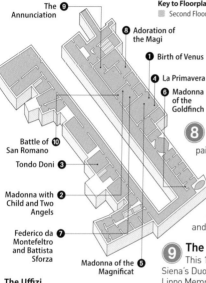

The Annunciation **9**

8 Adoration of the Magi

1 Birth of Venus

4 La Primavera

6 Madonna of the Goldfinch

Battle of San Romano **10**

Tondo Doni **3**

Madonna with Child and Two Angels **2**

Federico da Montefeltro and Battista Sforza **7**

Madonna of the Magnificat **5**

Key to Floorplan
▦ Second Floor

The Uffizi

8 Adoration of the Magi

This large work (1423), painted in tempera on wood by Gentile da Fabriano, is one of the masterpieces of the International Gothic style, with its sumptuous colours, depiction of elegant clothes and a fairy-tale atmosphere.

9 The Annunciation

This 1333 panel was painted for Siena's Duomo by Simone Martini and Lippo Memmi. The Virgin's expression – almost surprise or fear – gives the work a great sense of reality. The delicate, elegant lines and colours make this a Sienese Gothic masterpiece.

NEED TO KNOW

MAP M4–N4 ▪ Piazzale degli Uffizi 6 (off Piazza della Signoria) ▪ 055 294 883 (reservations) ▪ www.uffizi.it

Open 8:15am–6:30pm Tue–Sun; closed 1 Jan & 25 Dec

Adm €20

▪ Take a break at the outdoor café at the end of the west wing galleries, above the Loggia de' Lanzi.

▪ Avoid notoriously long queues by booking ahead or online – it's well worth paying the small fee.

▪ The Uffizi is undergoing major expansion and exhibits are likely to change location. Inquire at the gallery or check online for an update.

10 Battle of San Romano

A master of perspective, Uccello experimented with it to the detriment of the scene. The lances in this **(above)** third of his 1456 masterpiece (the other pieces are in Paris and London) over-define a perspective plane, while the background tilts at a radical angle.

The Uffizi Collections

Masaccio's *Sant'Anna Metterza*

of the Shepherds by Van der Goes are in Room 15, which is now called the Hugo Van der Goes Room. Compare this *Adoration* with those by Botticelli's student, Filippino Lippi, and by Botticelli's contemporary (and Michelangelo's teacher), Ghirlandaio.

① Early Renaissance
(Rooms 7–9)

The earthiness of Masaccio and the delicacy of Fra Angelico join the likes of Paolo Uccello in rooms 7 to 9. Renaissance ideals develop further with anatomically exacting works by the Pollaiuolo brothers and the flowing lines of Masaccio's elegant student Filippo Lippi, whose *Madonna with Child and Two Angels* is here (see p12). These lead up to the languid grace of Lippi's protégé, Botticelli.

② Botticelli
(Rooms 10–14 and 15)

Tear your eyes away from the famed *La Primavera* (see p12) and *Birth of Venus* to admire other Botticelli masterpieces such as *Pallas and the Centaur*. His *Adoration of the Magi* featuring a self-portrait (in yellow robes on the right) and *Adoration*

③ Pre-Renaissance
(Rooms 3–7)

The first Uffizi room bridges the medieval and proto-Renaissance with a trio of *Maestàs*, from Cimabue's Byzantine work through Duccio's Sienese Gothic style to Giotto's version. Simone Martini's *Annunciation* (see p13) represents the graceful 14th-century Sienese School. Gentile da Fabriano and Lorenzo Monaco give one final, colourful shout of the medieval in the International Gothic style of the early 15th century.

④ Leonardo da Vinci
(Rooms 29 and 35)

Rooms 29 and 35 celebrate some of Verrocchio's star pupils, including Lorenzo di Credi, Umbrian master Perugino (Raphael's teacher), Botticini and Leonardo da Vinci himself. As an apprentice, Leonardo painted the angel on the left of Verrocchio's *Baptism of Christ*. Leonardo da Vinci's restored *Annunciation* and his unfinished, chaotic *Adoration of the Magi* round out the room.

⑤ High Renaissance and Mannerism
(Room 38)

Michelangelo's *Tondo Doni*

After some Peruginos, Signorellis and a Venetian interlude, Room 38 marks the start of the High Renaissance, with Michelangelo's *Tondo Doni*. Andrea del Sarto and his students developed the colours and asymmetrical positioning of Michelangelo into Mannerism. Precise compositions by Raphael are also on display here.

⑥ European Masters (Rooms 28–35)

Opened in 2011, this display is part of the Uffizi's vast collection of non-Italian works, in rooms that were severely damaged by a bomb in 1993. The display includes significant 16th- to 18th-century Spanish works by Goya and Velázquez. Portraits by Rembrandt van Rijn and works by Rubens can be found in Room 34, while El Greco's paintings hang in Room 20.

⑦ Baroque (Rooms 29–32)

The post-Renaissance collections at the Uffizi are not outstanding, save for a few works by Caravaggio – a *Sacrifice of Isaac*, *Medusa* and *Bacchus*. The last is typical of his realistic style. He depicts the deity as a common man. Of his followers, so-called *caravaggeschi* works include *Judith Beheading Holofernes* by Artemisia Gentileschi, the first woman to become a member of the Accademia delle Arti del Disegno.

⑧ The Tribune (Room 4)

The Uffizi's original display space is a room decorated with mother-of-pearl and inlaid *pietre dure*, built by Francesco I to show off the *Medici Venus* and other classical statues. Portraits by Bronzino and Pontormo, Rosso Fiorentino's lute-plucking *Musician Angel* and Raphael's *St John in the Desert* cover the walls.

⑨ U-Shaped Corridor

The second-floor main corridor linking the galleries is lined with statues. These are mostly Roman copies of Greek originals. Its ceiling vaults are frescoed (1581) with grotesques depicting Florence's history, leaders, thinkers and artists. The views from the short south corridor are celebrated.

Boy with Thorn, U-Shaped Corridor

⑩ Vasari Corridor

The 1-km (0.6-mile) corridor between the Pitti Palace and the Palazzo Vecchio, passing through the Uffizi and lined with various works from the 17th to 20th centuries, was damaged during a 1993 terrorist bombing. Undergoing restoration work, the corridor is scheduled to open to the public for tours in 2021.

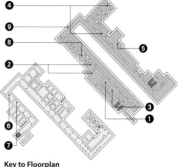

Key to Floorplan
First Floor
Second Floor

The Uffizi Collections

Bacchus by Caravaggio

TOP 10 ⭐ The Duomo Group, Florence

Florence's gorgeous cathedral offers two panoramic views, one atop Giotto's lithe and lovely bell tower, the other at the summit of Brunelleschi's robust and noble dome. The interior of the cathedral contains some Uccello frescoes but otherwise is oddly barren and less interesting than clambering up between the layers of the dome. The nearby Baptistry is also more rewarding with its glinting Byzantine mosaics and *Gates of Paradise,* while inside the museum are statues by Michelangelo, Donatello, Ghirlandaio and Pisano.

Duomo: Dome ③

The crossing of this Duomo **(right)** was thought to be unspannable until 1420 when Brunelleschi found an ingenious double shell solution. Forget the frescoes inside; climb between the layers to the marble lantern at its peak for a thrill.

① Baptistry: Gates of Paradise

Lorenzo Ghiberti's gilded bronze panels (1425–52) showcase his mastery at depicting great depth in shallow relief **(above)**. Reportedly, Michelangelo was so moved he proclaimed they would "grace the very gates of Paradise", and the name stuck. The original doors are housed in the Museo dell'Opera del Duomo.

④ Duomo: Fresco of Giovanni Acuto

Master of perspective, Paolo Uccello painted this trompe l'oeil fresco (1436) of an equestrian statue as a memorial for John Hawkwood, an English *condottiero* (mercenary leader) long in Florence's employ.

② Duomo: New Sacristy

The bronze doors and glazed terracotta lunette are 15th-century works by Luca della Robbia. The interior, sheathed in wood inlay, was where Lorenzo de' Medici took refuge after an assassination attempt in 1478.

⑤ Duomo: Campanile

Giotto designed only the lowest level of the "Lily of Florence" **(left)**, which was continued by Andrea Pisano and finished by Francesco Talenti. It is 85 m (276 ft), or 414 steps, to the top.

6 Baptistry: Mosaics

The 13th-century mosaic panels (above) here tell stories from Genesis and the lives of Jesus, Joseph and St John the Baptist.

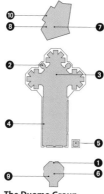

The Duomo Group

8 Museo dell'Opera del Duomo: Habakkuk

One of several prophets Donatello carved for the Campanile, this one was nicknamed *Lo Zuccone* – "Pumpkinhead" – by irreverent Florentines.

9 Baptistry: North Doors

Lorenzo Ghiberti won the 1401 competition to cast these 28 bronze panels, and spent 21 years creating what art historians consider the first proper Renaissance work.

10 Museo dell'Opera: Michelangelo's Pietà

Michelangelo created three *Pietàs*; the second of these (below) in 1548–55, which he later attacked in frustration.

7 Museo dell'Opera del Duomo: Altar Front

This ornate silver and gilt scene for the Baptistry took Verrocchio, Antonio Pollaiuolo, Michelozzo and other sculptors over 100 years to craft, from 1366 to 1480.

DUOMO HISTORY

Florence's Baptistry was probably founded in the 6th century, but its structure is 11th- to 14th-century. The cathedral wasn't started until 1294, when Arnolfo di Cambio began building around the old Santa Reparata (adm; reached via a crypt in the cathedral); it was largely finished by 1417. Brunelleschi's engineering added the dome in 1436, which was topped in the 1460s by Verrocchio's bronze. The Neo-Gothic façade is 19th-century.

NEED TO KNOW

MAP M3–N3 ■ Piazza del Duomo

Duomo: open 10:15am–4:45pm Mon–Sat; closed Sun

Dome: open 8:15am–7:30pm Mon–Fri (until 5:15pm Sat) & 12:45–5:15pm Sun

Baptistry: open 11:15am–7:30pm Fri (from 8:15am Sat), 8:15am–1:30pm Sun

Campanile: open 8:15am–7:45pm daily

Museo dell'Opera del Duomo: open 9am–7:45pm daily

Adm €18 (combined ticket; valid for 48 hours from first usage)

■ I Fratellini *(see p86)* is a hole-in-the-wall serving glasses of wine and sandwiches to customers who eat standing outside.

■ The last ascent of the dome is one hour before closing; visits require booking. Tours are every 45 minutes.

TOP 10 ★ Pitti Palace, Florence

This one-time residence of the Medici family is a treasure-trove: there are royal apartments, galleries of modern art, costume, silverware and porcelain. Above all, there is the Galleria Palatina, frescoed by Pietro da Cortona, and second only to the Uffizi. It contains one of the world's best collections of Raphaels and Titians. The paintings are still hung 19th-century style, when "Does that Tintoretto match the room's decor?" or "Let's put all the round ones together" mattered more than any didactic arrangement.

2 La Velata
Raphael did many portraits, usually of Madonnas, and several of his best are in these collections. *La Velata* (1516) is his masterpiece **(left)** of portraiture, displaying his mastery of colour, light and form *(see p20)*. The sitter is most likely La Fornarina, his Roman girlfriend.

1 Mary Magdalene
This is the first (1535) of many Mary Magdalenes *(see p20)* painted by the Venetian master Titian.

3 Consequences of War
Venus tries to stop Mars from going to war, while Fate encourages him *(see p21)*. This was Rubens's plea against his country becoming embroiled in the Thirty Years' War.

The Pitti Palace exterior

4 Boboli Gardens
The Renaissance garden with Baroque and Rococo touches has cypress avenues, hidden statues and burbling fountains.

5 Three Ages of Man
The attribution of this allegorical work (1500) to Giorgione is not certain, but it is a beautiful piece *(see p20)* with strong colour and composition. Compare it to Pietro da Cortona's Baroque *Four Ages of Man* (1637), frescoed on the ceiling of the Sala della Stufa *(see p21)*.

6 Madonna and Child
In a masterful touch, Filippo Lippi placed the Madonna's chin in the geometric centre of this work **(below)**, helping to unite a complex composition *(see p21)* involving both the main scene and background images from the Virgin's life.

MUSEUM GUIDE

Enter via Ammannati's Courtyard (ticket office is to the right of Pitti Palace). Galleria Palatina and the royal apartments are on the first floor, but see the Palatina first. The Boboli entrance is in the back right-hand corner. The other collections are: Modern Art Gallery; Costume Gallery (in the Meridiana Summer Palace); Silver Collection (ground floor); Porcelain Museum (at the top of the Boboli); Carriage Museum (left wing, call 055 2388 611 before visiting).

7 Grotta Grande

This Mannerist cavern **(above)** is dripping with stylized stalactites, Giambologna statues and plaster casts of Michelangelo's *Slaves*.

8 Ammannati's Courtyard

Mannerist architecture was a robust, oversized take on the Renaissance. Bartolomeo Ammannati expounded this in dramatic, heavily rusticated Classical orders in this *cortile* (1560–70).

9 The Tuscan Maremma

On the second floor (not shown on the floorplan), the modern art gallery's jewel is Giovanni Fattori's 1850 work. He was the best of the Macchiaioli, a 19th-century Tuscan school with parallels with Impressionism.

10 Green Room, the Royal Apartments

The best-preserved room in the *Appartamenti Reali* contains lavish furnishings, such as an ebony cabinet inlaid with semi-precious stones and bronze. The ceiling of the Green Room is decorated with trompe l'oeil stuccoes and a canvas by Luca Giordano.

NEED TO KNOW

MAP L5 ■ Piazza de' Pitti

Galleria Palatina and Appartamenti Reali: 055 294 883; open 8:15am–6:30pm Tue–Sun; closed 1 Jan & 25 Dec

Galleria del Costume: open 8:30am–6:30pm; closed Mon, 1 Jan, 1 May & 25 Dec

Museo della Porcellana, Museo degli Argenti and Boboli Gardens: open Nov–Feb: 8:15am–4:30pm daily (Mar & Oct with winter clock: until 5:30pm; Apr–May, Sep & Oct with daylight saving: until 6:30pm; Jun–Aug: until 7:10pm); closed 1st & last Mon of the month, 1 Jan & 25 Dec; adm (Ticket includes adm to Garden of Villa Bardini)

■ Pitti Gola e Cantina (see p86), just across the piazza, offers light meals and snacks.

■ The gardens surrounding the palace are a good spot for a picnic.

■ You can buy a modern version of Pitti Palace's *pietre dure* table (see p21) at Pitti Mosaici on the Piazza de' Pitti.

Pitti Palace

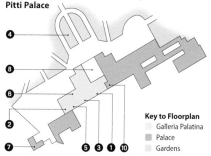

Key to Floorplan
- Galleria Palatina
- Palace
- Gardens

Pitti Palace: Galleria Palatina

Giorgione's *Three Ages of Man*

1 Sala di Giove

This room holds two of Pitti's top sights: Raphael's *La Velata* and Giorgione's *Three Ages of Man (see p18)*. Early Renaissance masterpieces include Perugino's *Madonna del Sacco*, a subtle study of spatial relationships, and a small, wrinkly *St Jerome* either by Verrocchio or Piero di Pollaiuolo. Andrea del Sarto painted *St John the Baptist* (1523) in a classical style, but his *Annunciation* (1512) is proto-Mannerist. Fra Bartolomeo's *Lamentation of the Dead Christ* (1512) and Bronzino's *Guidobaldo Della Rovere* (1532) are High Renaissance works that anticipate the Baroque.

2 Sala di Saturno

Raphael's entire career is covered here, from the Leonardesque *Madonna del Granduca* (1506) to his late *Vision of Ezekiel* (1518). While his other Madonnas and portraits are here, the Mona Lisa-inspired *Maddalena Doni* (1506), which heavily influenced Renaissance portraiture, is displayed in the Uffizi. Raphael's teacher Perugino painted a strikingly composed *Lamentation of the Dead Christ* (1495). Fra Bartolomeo's *Stupor Mundi* (1516) and del Sarto's *Annunciation and Dispute of the Trinity* (1517) round out the room.

3 Sala di Apollo

Titian finds a home here: his *Mary Magdalene (see p18)* hangs near his *Portrait of an Englishman* (1540). Influential works abound: Andrea del Sarto's *Pietà* (1522) and *Holy Family* (1523) helped found the Mannerist style. The tight, focused power of the *Sacred Conversation* (1522), by del Sarto's student Rosso Fiorentino, was affected when the painting was later artificially extended to fit a large Baroque frame. The classical style of Bolognese artists Guido Reni (a late *Cleopatra*) and Guercino (an early *Resurrection of Tabitha*) helped inform the burgeoning Baroque.

4 Sala di Venere

The centrepiece of the room is a *Venus* carved by Canova to replace the ancient original Napoleon had shipped back to Paris (it is now in the Uffizi). Titian steals the show with *The Concert* (1510; Giorgione may also have contributed), a *Portrait of Julius II* (1545) copied from Raphael and the celebrated *Portrait of Pietro Aretino* (1545). Rubens's bucolic work *Return from the Hayfields* is often overlooked.

5 Sala dell'Educazione di Giove

There are two works of particular note in this room: Caravaggio's *Sleeping Cupid* (1608) is a study in realism and chiaroscuro. Cristofano Allori's *Judith Beheading Holofernes* has double meanings: every face in it is a portrait from life. Judith is the artist's girlfriend, the old woman looking on bears the face of her mother and the decapitated head of Holofernes is Cristofano Allori's self-portrait.

Venus, Sala di Venere

6 Later Works

Some of the rest can't live up to the highlights, though the names – Tintoretto, Botticelli, Rubens, Pontormo – remain major. The only masterworks are Raphael's *Madonna dell'Impannata* (1514) and a 1450 Filippo Lippi *Madonna and Child* (see p18), the museum's oldest painting. Compare Signorelli's *Sacra Famiglia* displayed in the Uffizi, which influenced Michelangelo's, with that of Beccafumi – a Mannerist take informed by the work of Michelangelo.

7 Sala dell'Iliade

Raphael's unusual, almost Flemish-style portrait of a pregnant woman, *La Gravida* (1506), is the star of the room. Andrea del Sarto is represented by a pair of *Assumptions* (painted 1523 and 1526). Artemisia Gentileschi is also represented: she is one of the most famous female artists from the Baroque period (see p15) and often portrayed strong female biblical characters, including Mary Magdalene and Judith, in her works.

8 Sala di Marte

Rubens dominates with the 1638 *Consequences of War* (see p18) and *Four Philosophers* (1612), which includes portraits of himself (far left) and his brother. The fine collection includes the penetrating *Portrait of a Man* (1550), which is attributed to

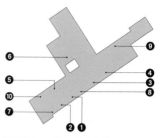

Pitti Palace: Galleria Palatina

Paolo Veronese, *Luigi Cornaro* (1560), which is now attributed to Tintoretto, *Ippolito de' Medici* (1532) by Titian and *Cardinal Bentivoglio* by Van Dyck.

9 Galleria delle Statue

Paintings are on temporary display in this long entrance hall, but a few have been here for years, such as Caravaggio's violent genre scene *The Toothpuller* (officially an Uffizi painting) and an early Rubens *Risen Christ*. Don't miss the 19th-century table which is a fine example of *pietre dure*, the art of inlaid stone.

10 Sala della Stufa and Napoleon's Bathroom

The Sala della Stufa preserves Pietro da Cortona frescoes and 1640 majolica flooring. Napoleon's Empire-style bathroom is one of the few Pitti Palace remnants of the Frenchman's brief Italian reign.

Consequences of War by Rubens in the Sala di Marte

TOP 10 ⭐ San Gimignano

Souvenir shops notwithstanding, this pedestrianized hill town is the most evocative of the Middle Ages of any in Tuscany. This UNESCO World Heritage Site is nicknamed San Gimignano delle Belle Torri, or San Gimignano of the Beautiful Towers. Over 70 of these towers once attested to this medieval Manhattan's wealth; 14 still spike its skyline today. The town has, for its size, a wealth of 14th- and 15th-century art. Modern art, too, is tucked into unexpected corners, and there is an excellent local white wine.

1 Collegiata

The plain exterior belies an interior covered in frescoes **(below)**. The ones on the right wall are by Lippo Memmi (1333–41), and those on the left by Bartolo di Fredi (1367). Taddeo di Bartolo painted the gory *Last Judgement* (1410) inside the nave and Benozzo Gozzoli created *St Sebastian* (1464) on the entrance wall. The town's pride are the fascinating Domenico Ghirlandaio frescoes (1475) in the Chapel of Santa Fina.

The atmospheric hill town of San Gimignano

3 Museo Civico

San Gimignano's best museum is situated on the first floor of the Palazzo Comunale, beneath the lofty Torre Grossa. The collection includes the 1511 work *Madonna with Saints Gregory and Benedict* by Pinturicchio, a *Maestà* by Lippo Memmi and works by Filippino Lippi and Benozzo Gozzoli. Memmo di Filuppucci's 14th-century frescoes depicting a couple's marriage and their wedding night are unusually erotic for the period.

2 Torre Grossa

You can climb all 54 m (175 ft) of the tallest tower in town for one of Italy's most stupendous views, across the surrounding towers and terracotta roofs to the rolling hills all around.

4 Museo della Tortura

A grisly array of torture instruments occupies the Torre della Diavola or She-Devil's Tower **(right)**. The explanatory placards make for grim reading, pointing out which of the devices are still used around the world today.

Previous pages The city as seen from Museo dell'Opera, Siena

5 Façade of San Francesco

The Romanesque façade of this long-vanished church remains wedged between later medieval buildings. Behind it is a local vineyard's *cantina*, offering wine tastings and, beyond, a pretty, shaded terrace with fine country views.

6 Sant'Agostino

Most tourists miss this little church **(right)** with its 1483 Piero di Pollaiuolo altarpiece and Gozzoli's quirky, colourful apse frescoes on the life of St Augustine (1465). Benedetto da Maiano carved the tomb of San Bartolo (1488) against the west wall.

7 Museo d'Arte Sacra

This modest museum of liturgical art stands on a pretty piazza off the left flank of the Collegiata. Highlights of the collection are a *Madonna and Child* by Bartolo di Fredi and 14th-century illuminated choir books.

8 Rocca

The 14th-century fortress has long since crumbled to a romantic ruin, and is now planted with olive and fig trees. To get a picture-perfect view of the town's tall towers scramble up the fortress' ramparts.

SAN GIMIGNANO'S HISTORY

The Etruscan and later Roman settlement blossomed as a way-point on the medieval Via Francigena pilgrim route. Competing local families built the towers as a competitive display of wealth as well as for defence. A devastating plague, called the Black Death, swept through town in 1348, leaving it under Florentine control, and causing the pilgrim route to shift east. San Gimignano gradually became a backwater, its medieval character preserved to this day.

9 Museo Archeologico

The small collection of Etruscan artifacts here includes a curious funerary urn topped by a reclining effigy of the deceased, his cup holding a coin to pay for entry into the afterlife.

10 Piazza della Cisterna

This triangular piazza **(below)**, ringed with 13th- and 14th-century towers and centred on a 1237 stone well, will be familiar as a setting for such films as *Where Angels Fear to Tread* and *Tea with Mussolini*.

NEED TO KNOW

MAP D3

Visitor information: Piazza del Duomo 1; 0577 940 008; www.sangimignano.com

Collegiata: open daily; adm €5; www. duomosangimignano.it

Museo Civico: open daily; adm €9; www. sangimignanomusei.it

Museo della Tortura: open daily; adm €10; www.torturemuseum.it

Museo Archeologico: open daily; adm €9; www.sangimignanomusei.it

Museo d'Arte Sacra: opening hours vary, check website; adm €5; www.duomo sangimignano.it

■ Combined tickets for all sights are available from the tourist office.

■ The opening times of museums often vary; it's advisable to check online or with the tourist office.

TOP 10 ★ Piazza del Duomo, Pisa

Pisa's UNESCO World Heritage Site is one of Italy's most gorgeous squares, its green carpet of grass the setting for the Pisan-Romanesque gemstones of the Duomo, Camposanto, Baptistry and Campanile – that icon better known as the Leaning Tower. The east end of the square is anchored by the old bishop's palace, now the Duomo museum. Souvenir stalls cling like barnacles to the square's south side; a doorway between them opens into the Museo delle Sinopie, housing the giant preparatory sketches on plaster for the lost Camposanto frescoes.

3 Leaning Tower

This bell tower in the Pisan-Romanesque style was begun in 1173 and started leaning when builders were only on the third level **(left)**. By 1990, the tower was 4.5 m (15 ft) out of vertical, and was closed for engineers to reverse the tilt. They announced in 2008 that it had been stabilized.

4 Duomo Façade

The façade is a triumph of blind arcades, stacked open arches and coloured marble decorations **(right)**. Giambologna cast the bronze doors to replace those destroyed by fire in 1595.

1 Duomo's San Ranieri Door

In 1180, Bonanno Pisano sculpted the only remaining Romanesque bronze door of Pisa's cathedral, gracing it with minimalist biblical scenes and palm trees. The original door is now in the Museo dell'Opera.

5 Museo delle Sinopie

Restorers discovered sketches for the lost Camposanto frescoes, offering an insight into the creative process of these medieval artists.

Duomo Pulpit 2

Nicola Pisano's son, Giovanni, carved this pulpit **(right)** in 1302–11. The Gothic naturalism visible in its tumultuous New Testament scenes most probably reflects the influence of Giotto, who was a contemporary working in Padua.

ORIENTATION

Piazza del Duomo is a 15- to 20-minute bus ride (take No 4 or the LAM Rossa) or a 20- to 25-minute walk from Pisa Centrale station in Piazza della Stazione. Admission to the sites is available in several configurations; currently these are as follows: a free ticket for the Duomo alone; €5 for any one site, €7 for two, €8 for three except the Tower; €18 for the Tower alone. The city walls are also accessed for free.

6 Museo dell'Opera del Duomo

The rich collection at this museum includes an 11th-century Islamic bronze hippogriff (half horse, half griffin). Taken in a Crusade, this once topped the cathedral dome.

Piazza del Duomo

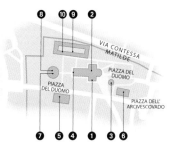

7 Baptistry

Italy's largest Baptistry started life as a Romanesque piece (1153) but has a Gothic dome. The acoustically perfect interior houses a great Gothic pulpit by sculptor Nicola Pisano.

8 Baptistry Pulpit

Nicola Pisano's Gothic masterpiece (1255–60) depicts a number of religious scenes based on ancient pagan reliefs decorating the sarcophagi in the Camposanto.

9 Camposanto

This former cemetery, which contains recycled Roman sarcophagi, once featured frescoes to rival those in the Sistine Chapel, such as this one by Buffalmacco **(below)**. Although largely destroyed in World War II, a few sections are preserved in a back room.

NEED TO KNOW

MAP C3

Visitor information: Piazza del Duomo 7: 050 550 100, www.turismo.pisa.it (tickets: www.opapisa.it)

Duomo: open daily; a free pass from the ticket office is required for entry

Leaning Tower: open daily; adm €20

Baptistry: open daily; adm €7

Camposanto: open daily; adm €7

Museo dell'Opera del Duomo: open daily; adm €7

Museo delle Sinopie: open daily; adm: €7

■ Head to Il Canguro (*Via Santa Maria 151*) for a quick and tasty lunch break.

■ The opening times of sites vary; check online or with the tourist office.

10 Camposanto Triumph of Death Fresco

This fresco by Buffalmacco is the best of those that survived World War II. Its scene of Death riding across an apocalyptic landscape inspired Liszt to compose his *Totentanz* concerto.

Other Pisan Sights

① Museo San Matteo

Often-overlooked collection of 13th-century Crucifixions and such notable works as Simone Martini's *Virgin and Child with Saints* (1321), Nino Pisano's *Madonna del Latte* and Donatello's bust of San Rossore. Masaccio, Fra Angelico, Gozzoli, Lorenzo di Credi and Ghirlandaio are also represented.

② Santa Maria della Spina

The church is a pinnacled jewel of Gothic architecture built in 1230–1323 by Nino and Giovanni Pisano to house a thorn said to be from Christ's crown, brought back by a Pisan Crusader.

Detail, Santa Caterina mosaic

③ Piazza Vettovaglie Market

This attractive arcaded piazza stands at the centre of Pisa's colourful, lively outdoor food market.

④ Piazza dei Cavalieri

The probable site of the ancient forum is ringed by Giorgio Vasari's *sgrafitto* façade on the Palazzo dei Cavalieri (1562), the Baroque Santo Stefano church and the Palazzo dell'Orologio. It was in the last's tower that Count Ugolino, immortalized by Dante and Shelley, was accused of treason in 1288 and locked away to starve with his sons.

⑤ Santa Caterina

Behind the 1330 Gothic façade hides Nino Pisano's sculpture *Annunciation* and his tomb of Simone Saltarelli (1342), as well as Francesco Triani's *Apotheosis of St Thomas Aquinas* (1350).

⑥ Le Navi Antiche di Pisa

Thirty Roman ships, dating from 100 BC to AD 400 and probably sunk by flash floods or storms, were discovered in 1998 during work on San Rossore station (which was the harbour area before the Arno silted up). The ships' cargo and everyday accoutrements are being displayed in the Medici Arsenale as they are excavated, and will eventually be joined by the ships themselves.

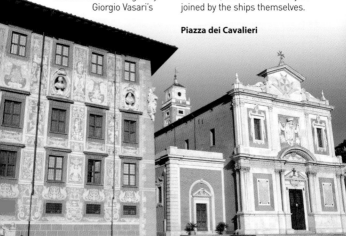

Piazza dei Cavalieri

Certosa di Calci monastery

7 Certosa di Calci

This Carthusian monastery, set 12 km (8 miles) east of town, dates to 1366 and features Baroque frescoed chapels and cloisters.

8 Tenuta di San Rossore

Boar, deer and waterfowl abound in this coastal wildlife reserve. The poet Shelley's body was washed ashore here in 1822 after his boat sank and he drowned in the Gulf of La Spezia.

9 San Paolo a Ripa d'Arno

This venerable church (805 AD) has a 13th-century façade and the Romanesque chapel of Sant'Agata is set in the grassy park behind.

10 San Nicola

Donato Bramante's Vatican steps were inspired by the bell tower stairs of this 1,000-year-old church.

THE LEANING TOWER

Italy's most famous symbol once leaned a staggering 4.5 m (15 ft) out of plumb. The problem: 55 m (180 ft) of marble stacked atop watery, alluvial sand. A worrisome list developed soon after building started in 1173. Work stopped until 1275, when it was decided to curve the tower back as it rose. By 1990, with over a million tourists annually tramping up the tower, collapse seemed imminent. The tower was closed, with restraining bands strapped around it, lead weights stacked on one side and the base excavated to try to reverse the lean. It eventually reopened at the end of 2001. A limited number of visitors are allowed and tickets are available at set times. Engineers and experts predicted in 2008 that the tower should remain stable for at least another 200 years.

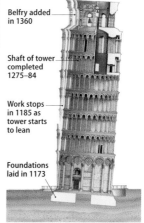

Belfry added in 1360

Shaft of tower completed 1275–84

Work stops in 1185 as tower starts to lean

Foundations laid in 1173

The tower rests on a stone platform. An attempt was made in 1836 to dig out the foundations, but the lean worsened so work stopped. Monitors placed in the soil below the foundations now track any movement.

PIAZZA DEL DUOMO

VIA S. ZENO

VIA B. PISANNO
VIA ROMA
VIA S. MARIA

VIA S. FRANCESCO

12 km (8 miles)

Arno

LUNG. MEDICEO
LUNG. GALILEO

CORSO ITALIA

LUNG. SONNINO

5 km (3 miles)

PIAZZA VITTORIO EMANUELE II

Other Pisan Sights

🔟 ⭐ Siena's Duomo

Siena's hulking Duomo is a treasure house of late Gothic sculpture, early Renaissance painting and Baroque design. Early architects dressed the edifice in striking Romanesque stripes, but its form is firmly Gothic, one of the best examples of the style in Italy. Equally fascinating are the Duomo's outbuildings: the Baptistry, the Museo dell'Opera Metropolitana and the Santa Maria della Scala hospital across the square, where 1440s frescoes in the wards depict medieval hospital scenes.

② Façade
Giovanni Pisano designed the façade **(left)** in 1285. His original time-worn statues (replaced now with copies) are in the Museo dell'Opera Metropolitana. The mosaics on the top half are by 19th-century Venetian craftsmen.

① Pisano Pulpit
Nicola Pisano's son, Giovanni, and his pupil Arnolfo di Cambio helped create this masterpiece of Gothic carving. Similar to Pisano pulpits in Pistoia and Pisa, it depicts scenes from the Life of Christ.

③ Piccolomini Altar
Andrea Bregno's 1480 marble altar incorporates a *Madonna and Child* (1397–1400) by Jacopo della Quercia and four small statues of saints (1501–4) by the young Michelangelo.

④ San Giovanni Chapel
Giovanni di Stefano's Renaissance baptismal chapel (1492) is decorated with Pinturicchio frescoes and a bronze *St John the Baptist* (1457) by an ageing Donatello.

DUOMO HISTORY

The Duomo was largely built between 1215 and 1263 by, among others, Nicola Pisano. His son Giovanni designed the façade. In 1339, work began on a huge new nave. The idea was to turn the Duomo we see today into merely the transept of the largest church in Christendom. This plan was thwarted by the Black Death in 1348, and the would-be façade is now a terrace, while the unfinished nave wall now houses the cathedral museum.

⑤ Floor Panels
All 59 panels are on show in early autumn (usually late June to October), but some are visible all year. Between 1372 and 1547, these exquisite marble mosaics **(left)** were created by Siena's top artists, including Pinturicchio and Matteo di Giovanni, whose *Massacre of the Innocents* is masterful.

6 Duccio's Stained-Glass Window

Italy's earliest stained glass (1288) decorates the round window in the apse. Designed by Siena's great early Gothic master Duccio di Boninsegna, it underwent a thorough cleaning in the 1990s. The original has now been placed in the cathedral museum, the Museo dell'Opera Metropolitana.

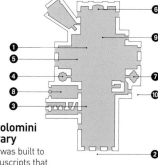

Siena's Duomo

8 Piccolomini Library

The library was built to house manuscripts that belonged to the humanist Pope Pius II, born to Siena's Piccolomini family. His life is celebrated in masterly frescoes by Pinturicchio (left) that date from 1502 to 1507.

9 Choir

The intarsia wood choir stalls were made by various master craftsmen (1362–1570), the 1532 marble altar by Baldassarre Peruzzi, the angel candelabra (c.1488) by Francesco di Giorgio Martini and the apse *Ascension* fresco by Beccafumi from 1548 to 1551.

7 Chigi Chapel

Baroque master Gian Lorenzo Bernini designed this chapel in 1659. The 13th-century *Madonna del Voto* altarpiece is Siena's guardian angel: officials have placed the city keys before her in times of crisis, including during Nazi occupation, and Siena has always been delivered from harm.

NEED TO KNOW

MAP E4 ■ Piazza del Duomo 8 ■ 0577 283 048 ■ www.opera-duomo.siena.it

Duomo, library, crypt, museum, baptistry: 10am–7pm daily (Nov–Mar: until 5:30pm); late Dec–early Jan: 10:30am–6pm daily

Santa Maria della Scala: 10:30am–7pm daily

Adm €8 for Duomo, €13 Duomo, library, museum, crypt, baptistry combined (€20 with roof access)

■ A nearby bakery, Il Magnifico (see p97), has been making traditional Sienese pastries for three generations.

■ Preparatory drawings are on display at the Pinacoteca (see p95).

■ Check the Duomo website or call 0577 286 300 for information regarding ticket details.

10 Campanile

The tower (left) was added in 1313, but, with its dramatic black-and-white stripes, the design is Romanesque.

Sights on the Piazza del Duomo

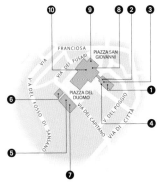

Sights on the Piazza del Duomo

1 Museo dell'Opera Metropolitana: Duccio's Maestà

The heavyweight masterpiece of Sienese Gothic painting. When Duccio finished it in 1311, Siena's citizens paraded it through the streets to the Duomo's altar.

2 Museo dell'Opera Metropolitana: Madonna and Child

This is Donatello's *schiacciato* master-piece, combining an etched perspective background with distorted (when seen close up) high relief to create an illusion of depth in a nearly flat surface.

Madonna and Child

3 Museo dell'Opera Metropolitana: Panorama from the Façade

The museum inhabits what would have been the nave wall of the aborted expansion *(see p30)*. Climb tight spiral stairs for great views.

4 Museo dell'Opera Metropolitana: Birth of the Virgin

This richly coloured, highly detailed Gothic work by Pietro Lorenzetti

uses real arches to introduce trompe l'oeil painted ceiling vaults, creating a sense of deep space.

5 Santa Maria della Scala: Pellegrinaio

This ward in the former civic hospital features scenes painted in the 1440s by Domenico di Bartolo, including monks tending the sick. The sym-bolic orphans climbing a *scala* (ladder) to heaven are by Vecchietta.

6 Santa Maria della Scala: Museo Archeologico

The small but worthwhile collection includes Greek vases from Southern Italy, Etruscan bronzes and alabaster urns, and Roman coins.

7 Santa Maria della Scala: Fonte Gaia

The weathered remnants of Jacopo della Quercia's original Fonte Gaia sculptures (1409–19) have been removed from the Campo *(see p34)* to their own atmospheric gallery.

8 Baptistry: Ceiling Frescoes

Gaze heavenwards in the Baptistry and marvel at the dense frescoes by Vecchietta (1440s); note the inclu-sion of such delightful and whimsical details as a monstrous crocodile.

9 Baptistry: Font

The brilliant bronze *Life of the Baptist* panels (1417–30) were cast by leading Florentine and Sienese sculptors that included Donatello and Ghiberti.

10 Duomo: Crypt

The frescoed chamber below the cathedral floor was only rediscovered in 2000. It is still uncertain who painted what, but everything dates to the late 1200s.

MIRACLES AND RELICS

The church of Santa Maria della Spina

Countless miracles have punctuated history in this fervently Christian land of saints and holy relics. When the crucifix in the church of Santa Trinita in Florence nodded its head in 1028 to Giovanni Gualberto, a local nobleman, he was moved to become a monk; he went on to found the Vallombrosan monastic order. The miraculous powers of the Madonna panel in a Florence granary and a Prato prison assured the buildings' transformations into the churches of Orsanmichele and Santa Maria delle Carceri. When the Crusader who brought the Virgin's girdle back to Prato hid it under his mattress, angels levitated his bed, retrieved the relic and flew it to the bishop. San Galgano even has a sword in the stone, plunged there by a soldier after St Michael appeared to him, ordering him to renounce his warrior ways and become a holy hermit.

TOP 10
RELICS IN TUSCANY

1 Virgin's Girdle (Prato, Duomo, *see p55*)

2 Volto Santo (Lucca, Duomo)

3 Thorn from Christ's Crown (Pisa, Santa Maria della Spina)

4 Madonna del Voto (Siena, Duomo)

5 Head of St Catherine (Siena, San Domenico)

6 Crucifix (Florence, Santa Trinita)

7 Piece of the True Cross (Impruneta, Collegiata)

8 Sword in the Stone (San Galgano, *see p116*)

9 Rib of a Dragon (Tirli)

10 Galileo's Finger (Florence, Science Museum)

The journey by boat of the girdle said to have been worn by the Virgin is depicted here. The country that gave the world Roman Catholicism is rich in many such artifacts that are imbued with miraculous qualities.

TOP 10 ★ Siena's Campo and Palazzo Pubblico

The Piazza del Campo, affectionately called Il Campo, is one of Europe's loveliest squares, where locals turn up to stroll and gossip. It has been the centre of Sienese public life since it was laid out atop the city's Roman Forum in 1100. The governmental Palazzo Pubblico, with its graceful tower, was added in 1297, and the curve of brick buildings opposite built to match. The Palazzo houses the Museo Civico. Twice a year, the Campo is packed with crowds for the Palio.

3 Museo Civico: Fresco Cycle

Ambrogio Lorenzetti's *Allegory of Good and Bad Government* (left), the greatest secular medieval fresco cycle in Europe, decorates the old city council chamber.

4 Museo Civico: Guidoriccio da Fogliano

This 1330 fresco (see p36) is Simone Martini's greatest – though some challenge its authorship. The austere Maremma landscape, where the nobleman Guidoriccio da Fogliano has just quashed the Montemassi rebellion, is charming.

1 Piazza del Campo

The square's nine sections honour the medieval ruling Council of Nine. Its fountain and slope are more than decorative: they're integral to the city's water system.

2 Palazzo Sansedoni

The oldest building (below) on the Campo, its curving 13th-century façade set the style for the rest of the square.

5 Palazzo Pubblico

With its graceful brickwork, three-light windows and medieval crenellations, the civic palace (1297–1310) set the standard for Sienese architecture. Its rooms now host the Museo Civico (see p36).

SIENA'S CONTRADE

The Campo is common ground for Siena's 17 traditional *contrade*, or wards. The Sienese are citizens of their *contrada* first, Siena second and Italy third. They are baptized in the *contrada* church, and should marry within their *contrada*; the *contrada* helps them in business, acts as their social club and mourns their deaths like family. The *contrade* do not tolerate crime, giving the town one of Europe's lowest crime rates. *Contrade* rivalries are played out here in the annual Palio horse race (see p77).

6 Loggia della Mercanzia

A commercial tribunal once held court under this 1417 loggia, which is decorated with sculptures by Vecchietta and Federighi. The tribunal judges were so famously impartial that governments from across Europe brought their financial disputes to be heard here.

Siena's Campo and Palazzo Pubblico

10 Torre del Mangia

At 102 m (336 ft), this is one of the tallest medieval towers in Italy (left). There are 503 steps to the top – worth the effort for the stunning view.

> **NEED TO KNOW**
>
> **MAP E4**
>
> *Visitor information:* Piazza del Campo 56; 0577 292 111; www.comune.siena.it
>
> *Palazzo Pubblico:* open 10am–7pm (winter: until 6pm); closed 25 Dec; adm €10
>
> *Torre del Mangia:* open 10am–1:45pm & 2–7pm daily (Nov–Feb: until 4pm); closed 25 Dec; adm €10
>
> *Palazzo Piccolomini:* open 10am, 11am & noon daily (by guided tour only)
>
> ■ Sip a cappuccino outdoors at one of the cafés around the Campo. Or try Nannini *(see p98)*, Siena's top café, just north of the Campo.
>
> ■ Behind the Palazzo Pubblico, Gino Cacino di Angelo *(Piazza Mercato 31)* is a great deli for buying snacks.
>
> ■ For details on events and exhibits in Siena, visit www.sienacomunica.it.

7 Palazzo Piccolomini

Housed in Siena's only Florentine Renaissance palace are the "Tavolette di Biccherna", municipal ledgers dating back to the 13th century, with covers by artists such as Ambrogio Lorenzetti, Sano di Pietro, Domenico Beccafumi and others.

8 Cappella della Piazza

When the Black Death of 1348 finally abated, the third of Sienese citizens who survived built this marble loggia, with detailed, pretty stone carvings, to give thanks for their deliverance – and to pray against a repeat of the plague.

9 Fonte Gaia

The felicitous "Fountain of Joy" (left) is pretty, but it is merely a mediocre 19th-century reproduction of the original, whose weathered carvings by Jacopo della Quercia are now housed in the Santa Maria della Scala *(see p32)*.

Siena's Museo Civico

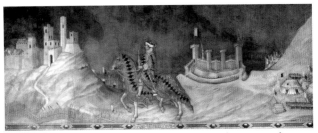

Simone Martini's fresco *Guidoriccio da Fogliano*, Sala del Mappamondo

① Sala del Mappamondo
Across from Simone Martini's *Guidoriccio da Fogliano* (see p34) is his impressive *Maestà* (1315). Among the frescoes is a monochrome 15th-century battle scene.

② Sala della Pace
Contains medieval Europe's greatest secular fresco by Lorenzetti (see p34), full of everyday life details.

Lorenzetti fresco, Sala della Pace

③ Cappella
This evocative room was frescoed by the Siennese pre-Renaissance artist Taddeo di Bartolo. Beyond an ornate screen is a fine altarpiece by Sodoma.

④ Anticappella
Taddeo di Bartolo also worked on the antechapel from 1415. His theme was civic virtue.

⑤ Sala di Balìa
Spinello Aretino and his son teamed up (1407–8) to illustrate the life of Pope Alexander III, featuring a fantastic naval battle.

⑥ Sala del Risorgimento
The room features 19th-century sculptures and murals on the life of King Vittorio Emanuele II, who unified Italy.

⑦ Sala del Concistoro
Delegates attended government meetings held beneath the ceiling frescoes by Beccafumi until 1786.

⑧ Anticamera del Concistoro
An Ambrogio Lorenzetti fresco is among the treasures here.

⑨ Vestibule
This is only a passageway, but it houses a 1429 gilded bronze she-wolf honouring Siena's Roman origins and a fresco by Ambrogio Lorenzetti.

⑩ Cortile del Podestà
The courtyard is decorated with a diverse array of ancient coats of arms.

Siena's Museo Civico

SIENESE ART

Birth of the Virgin by Pietro Lorenzetti

For a short time, Siena was as much a centre of artistic innovation as Florence, but sadly it was not destined to play such a big part in the Renaissance. Late 13th-century Sienese art came into its own as artists such as the painter Duccio started softening and enlivening the prevailing static Byzantine style with Gothic flowing lines and expressive features. By the early 14th century, Simone Martini and the Lorenzetti brothers were adding rich colour palettes and a penchant for intricate patterns to the mix. However, whereas Florence's Renaissance went on to revolutionize painting throughout Italy, the idiosyncratic Gothic style of Siena was dealt a crippling blow by the Black Death of 1348. The Lorenzettis died along with two-thirds of the population. A city concerned with rebuilding its economy and fending off Florentine expansion had no time or money for art. By the time Siena got back on its feet, local artists were following a variety of styles, from Gothic to Mannerist.

TOP 10
SIENESE ARTISTS

1 Simone Martini (1284–1344)

2 Duccio di Buoninsegna (1260–1319)

3 Ambrogio Lorenzetti (active 1319–48)

4 Pietro Lorenzetti (active 1306–48)

5 Domenico Beccafumi (1484–1551)

6 Sodoma (Giovanni Antonio Bazzi; 1477–1549)

7 Jacopo della Quercia (1371–1438)

8 Sassetta (1390–1450)

9 Francesco di Giorgio Martini (1439–1502)

10 Giovanni Duprè (1817–82)

Apparition on the Lake of Tiberiade is one of many scenes on the verso of Duccio's *Maestà* altarpiece, parts of which are now in Siena's cathedral museum.

TOP 10 ⭐ Chianti

The 50 km (30 miles) between Florence and Siena is a storybook landscape straight out of the background of a Renaissance painting: steeply rolling hills terraced with vineyards and olive groves, crenellated castles and bustling market towns. The seductive beauty of this Tuscan Arcadia has drawn people since Etruscan times; indeed, today it is so popular with the English that it has earned the nickname Chiantishire.

Castello di Brolio **1**

A vineyard since 1007, Brolio **(right)** has been the soul of the Chianti region since the "Iron Baron" Bettino Ricasoli *(see p70)* perfected the Chianti wine formula in the 19th century.

2 Greve in Chianti

This town has become Chianti's unofficial capital. There are plenty of wine shops in the area, but the most popular spot is Falorni **(below)**, one of Italy's great butchers, stuffed with hanging prosciutto, aged cheeses and free samples.

3 Radda in Chianti

With the 15th-century Palazzo del Podestà on top, this is the only hilltop member of the Chianti League. It is studded with the coats of arms of past mayors and offers good views. There's a butcher/grocer's here as well: Luciano Porciatti.

4 Montefioralle

Hovering above Greve, this 14th-century hamlet, consists of a single circular street, two churches and fantastic views over the valley and on to the 10th-century Pieve di San Cresci church below the walls.

5 Ipogeo di Montecalvario

A perfect 6th-century-BC tomb, the Ipogeo di Montecalvario has four passages tunnelling into its burial chambers. Visitors pay no entrance fee.

6 Pieve di San Leolino

Just south of Panzano is this little Romanesque church with Sienese paintings **(right)** from the 13th–15th centuries and a pretty brick cloister.

7 Panzano in Chianti

This often overlooked town is the home of Dario Cecchini, arguably Italy's best butcher, and a couple of fine *enoteche*, where visitors can sample the local wines paired with snacks.

8 Castellina in Chianti

The most medieval of the Chianti League towns, this features a glowering Rocca fortress. Via della Volte, a tunnel-like road pierced by "windows" overlooking the countryside, was a soldiers' walk when this was Florence's last out post before Siena.

Chianti

GETTING AROUND

The classic Chianti route is the S222 from Florence to Castellina; either zip straight down to Siena or explore more (highly recommended) by heading east on the S429 through Radda and Gaiole before you turn south on the S408 for Siena. But that only takes in the highlights. To truly get a feel for Chianti, take the back roads to Passignano, Coltibuono and other towns off the beaten path. Infrequent bus services also connect the main towns.

9 Badia a Coltibuono

This abbey dating from AD 770 includes an 11th-century church, Lorenza de' Medici's cookery school (see p139) and a restaurant run by her son.

NEED TO KNOW

MAP E3

Visitor information: Piazza Giacomo Matteotti 10, Greve in Chianti; 0558 546 299

■ A good number of local vineyards *(see pp40–41)* host wine tastings with small snacks.

■ You can put together a picnic fit for the gods at butchers such as Falorni in Greve *(see p92)* and Porciatti in Radda.

■ Email or call in advance before visiting a vineyard: find out when they accept visitors, whether they offer tours (and if they're free), and ask if you need to book a tour or make a tasting appointment.

10 Badia a Passignano

The Antinori wine empire owns the vineyards around this 11th-century monastery (below), which holds Baroque paintings by Ridolfo Ghirlandaio and local boy Il Passignano in the San Michele chapel, plus a *Last Supper* fresco by Davide and Domenico Ghirlandaio.

Chianti Vineyards

1 Castello di Brolio
MAP E4 ■ 0577 7301
■ www.ricasoli.it

The estate *(see p70)* that invented modern Chianti Classico is back in the Ricasoli family's hands. Book tours in advance.

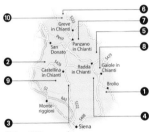

Chianti Vineyards

Castello di Brolio winery

2 Monsanto
MAP E3 ■ 0558 059 000
■ www.castellodimonsanto.it

This estate *(see p70)* makes a 100 per cent Sangiovese Chianti. Call to tour the cellars.

3 Fonterutoli
MAP E3 ■ 0577 741 385, 057 773 571 ■ www.mazzei.it

Highly regarded estate *(see p71)* in the Marquis Mazzei family since 1435. Excellent Chianti Classico, Badiola, Sangioveto and Morellino (in Belguardo). Tastings available.

4 Castello di Ama
MAP E3 ■ 0577 746 031, 0577 746 069 ■ www.castellodiama.com

Visitors can tour the estate, then taste and buy their wines at Rinaldi Palmira's *enoteca* in nearby Lecchi.

5 Castello di Volpaia
MAP E3 ■ 0577 738 066
■ www.volpaia.it

Visit the 13th-century village around an imposing central tower, and taste wines, oils and vinegars. Book tours a week ahead.

6 Castello Vicchiomaggio
MAP E3 ■ 055 854 079
■ www.vicchiomaggio.it

This enterprising estate offers tastings, cellar tours (notice required)

and cooking lessons on request. There is also a trattoria in the castle, and products also include olive oil.

7 Villa Vignamaggio
MAP E3 ■ 055 854 661
■ www.vignamaggio.com

A historic villa *(see p64)* whose wines were the first to be called Chianti. Book ahead for tours.

8 Villa Vistarenni
MAP E3 ■ 0577 738 476
■ www.villavistarenni.com

Modern cellars, a 17th-century villa and scenic vineyards, with tastings for small groups.

9 Rocca delle Macìe
MAP E3 ■ 0577 7321
■ www.roccadellemacie.com

A summer opera festival enlivens this estate, which also offers accommodation in 14th-century farm buildings.

10 Castello di Verrazzano
MAP E3 ■ 055 854 243
■ www.verrazzano.com

The family has been making wine since 1100. Sample it at the estate from Monday to Saturday.

Wine barrels, Castello di Verrazzano

THE STORY OF CHIANTI CLASSICO

Black Cockerel seal

Wine from the Chianti hills has been enjoyed at least since Roman times (one of its grapes, the Canaiolo, was cultivated by the Etruscans). It's been called Chianti since 1404, when a barrel was sent beyond the area to Prato. A political "Chianti League" of towns was formed in the 13th century, but it took a 1716 grand ducal decree to make this the world's first officially defined wine-producing region. In 1960, Chianti became the first Italian "DOCG" – the highest mark of quality. Some 70 sq km (27 sq miles) are strung with the grapes – two reds (Sangiovese and Canaiolo) and two whites (Malvasia and Trebbiano) – that make Chianti Classico. Though there are seven Chianti-producing regions, only wines produced in the Chianti hills may be called Classico and carry the seal of the Black Cockerel.

**TOP 10
RECENT VINTAGES**

1 2013
2 2010
3 2009
4 2008
5 2007
6 2006
7 2004
8 2001
9 1999
10 1997

Many vineyards allow visitors to sample their wares, and a bottle bought directly from the winery is a wonderful souvenir – or a treat for a picnic in the sun.

The villa and vineyards of the Villa Vistarenni estate

TOP 10 ⭐ Cortona

One of Tuscany's most rewarding hill towns, Cortona is a trove of Etruscan tombs, medieval alleyways, Renaissance art, sweeping views and small-town ambience. It was probably settled even before the Etruscans, and later became an important member of that society, as the tombs in its valley attest. The birthplace of Fra Angelico, Cortona also produced the Renaissance genius Luca Signorelli, the Baroque master Pietro da Cortona and the 20th-century Futurist Gino Severini.

Museo Diocesano ③

This small museum has outstanding works, from a Roman sarcophagus, studied by Donatello, to art by Pietro Lorenzetti, Fra Angelico, Francesco Signorelli and his uncle Luca, whose *Communion of the Apostles* (right) is held by the museum.

① Museo dell' Accademia Etrusca

This museum (above) was revamped in 2008 to expand the exhibits on Roman and Etruscan Cortona, including finds from the excavations at Melone del Sodo (I and II) plus a multimedia section. The star attraction in the original halls upstairs is a 5th-century-BC Medusa bronze lamp. The eclectic collection also includes paintings by Luca Signorelli and Pinturicchio, Egyptian finds and a section on Futurist Gino Severini.

San Niccolò ④

A tiny 15th-century church beyond a cypress-lined courtyard, housing a two-sided altarpiece by Luca Signorelli (ring the bell and ask the custodian to flip it for you).

Rugapiana (Via Nazionale) ⑤

The main drag of Cortona is the only flat street (*rugapiana* in local dialect) in town. Steep alleyways spill off from either side of this narrow, flagstoned, pedestrianized thoroughfare.

Melone I del Sodo ⑥

The passages of this 6th-century-BC Etruscan tomb were shored up in the 1800s. Visitors are also able to view the remarkable adjoining burial chambers and Etruscan script.

Duomo ②

A barrel-vaulted Renaissance cathedral (right), the Duomo is filled with paintings from the 16th and 17th centuries by Luca Signorelli and other artists.

7 Santa Maria delle Grazie al Calcinaio

An architectural set piece of the High Renaissance, Santa Maria (1485–1513) is the masterpiece of Francesco di Giorgio Martini, set amid olive groves below the town walls **(left)**.

CORTONA ORIENTATION

The road up to the hill town starts near the Melone tombs down on the valley floor. It winds up through olive groves, passing the Tomba di Pitagora and Santa Maria church, before terminating at the bus stop square of Piazza Garibaldi. From here, Via Nazionale leads into the heart of town – the piazzas Repubblica and Signorelli – close to most other sights.

10 Melone II del Sodo

The remarkable altar on this huge 6th-century-BC Etruscan tumulus was discovered in the 1990s. The altar – a sphinx-flanked staircase leading to a wide platform – is oriented towards Cortona up on the hillside, suggesting that this may have been the resting place of a prince.

NEED TO KNOW
MAP F4

Visitor information: Piazza Signorelli 9; 0575 637 274; www.cortonaweb.net

Museo dell'Accademia Etrusca: 0575 637 235; closed Mon & 25 Dec; adm €10; www.cortonamaec.org

Museo Diocesano: 0577 286 300; closed 25 Dec; adm €6; www.cortonatusei bellezza.it/museo-diocesano/

Melone del Sodo (I and II): 0575 630 415; open 10am–7pm Tue–Sun; closed Mon; adm €10; www.cortonamaec.org

■ Enoteca Enotria *(Via Nazionale 81)* offers laid-back wine tastings that are accompanied by cheese, local *ciaccia* (bread) and *salumi* (cured meats).

■ Follow Via Santa Margherita as it winds up past gardens and Severini-designed shrines to the 16th-century Fortezza Medicea di Girifalco for views over Val di Chiana to Lake Trasimeno.

8 San Domenico

The church features a faded Fra Angelico lunette fresco of the Madonna over the entrance, a Luca Signorelli *Madonna* inside, and a huge, glittering 15th-century Lorenzo di Niccolò altarpiece that is entirely intact (a rarity).

9 Tomba di Pitagora

The dirt hillock covering this 3rd-century-BC tomb **(below)** was removed long ago. The stone chamber was erroneously dubbed "Pythagoras' Tomb" when somebody confused Cortona with the mathematician's hometown, Crotone, in Calabria.

Etruscan Sights Around Cortona and Beyond

1 Cortona: Museo dell'Accademia Etrusca

Cortona's best museum *(see p42)* has a number of superb Etruscan and Cortonese artifacts.

2 Cortona: Tombs

Etruscan tombs *(see pp42–3)* in the valley below Cortona include the two "Melone" tombs, and the Tomba di Pitagora.

3 Volterra: Museo Etrusco Guarnacci

Etruscans transformed this 9th-century-BC town into part of the Dodecapolis confederation. Over 600 marvellous funerary urns fill the museum *(see p57)*, which also preserves the *Shade of the Evening*, an elegantly elongated bronze sculpture of a boy.

4 Sovana: Tombs and Vie Cave

Six necropolises surround this Etruscan settlement *(see p128)*, most of them romantically overgrown. The *vie cave* are narrow paths carved up to 20 m (65 ft) deep – their function is unknown.

5 Florence: Museo Archeologico

Along with riches from Ancient Rome and Antioch, Florence's oft-overlooked archaeology museum *(see p84)* preserves one of the greatest artworks from Etruria, a large, 4th-century-BC bronze chimera, probably cast in Chiusi or Orvieto.

6 Populonia

An ancient coastal smelting centre *(see p128)*, this medieval town has a small museum and some ancient walls. A nearby necropolis illustrates changing

Etruscan tomb in Populonia

tomb styles, from simple passages to domed tumuli (barrows) to *edicola* (shrine-type tombs).

7 Chiusi: Museo Archeologico Nazionale Etrusco

This excellent museum *(see p122)* houses fine jars and funerary urns, some with miraculously preserved polychrome paintings.

8 Chiusi: Tombs

A custodian from Chiusi museum will accompany you to unlock two of the tombs dotting Chiusi's valley *(see p122)*, including the Tomba della Pellegrina with its urns and sarcophagi still in place.

9 Grosseto: Museo Civico Archeologico

Many artifacts found in the Maremma (Sovana, Roselle, Vetulonia), such as terracotta reliefs and painted vases *(see p128)*, have made their way here.

Cooking pot, Grosseto

10 Roselle

The only fully excavated Etruscan town in Tuscany, Roselle was once part of Dodecapolis but was conquered early (294 BC). The remains of Etruscan walls and houses lie next to a Roman amphitheatre and baths.

THE ETRUSCANS

Tuscany is named after the Etruscans who settled central Italy, from Northern Lazio to the Umbrian Apennines, around the 8th century BC. Little is known about them beyond scant Roman records (the early Roman Tarquin kings were actually Etruscan) and the artifacts that have survived, of which most are funerary. According to myth, they came from Asia Minor (bringing with them Tuscany's familiar cypress tree), enjoyed an advanced culture, with relative equality between the sexes, and excelled at engineering – Etruscans taught the Romans the art of draining land for agriculture. They traded extensively with the Greeks, who had settled southern Italy; much Etruscan-era painted pottery is either Greek- or Attic-influenced, and the analphabetic Etruscans quickly adopted Greek letters. Their 12 greatest city-states formed a loose and somewhat fluctuating confederation called Dodecapolis. By the 3rd century BC, expansion-hungry Romans began conquering Etruria, replacing Etruscan hill towns with Roman valley camps and ruler-straight roads.

**TOP 10
TOWNS FOUNDED
BY THE ETRUSCANS**

1 Volterra (Map D4)
2 Arezzo (Map F3)
3 Chiusi (Map F5)
4 Cortona (Map F4)
5 Fiesole (Map E2)
6 Pitigliano (Map F6)
7 Sovana (Map F6)
8 Populonia (Map C5)
9 Saturnia (Map E6)
10 Roselle (Map E5)

Etruscan alabaster funerary urn in Volterra's Museo Etrusco Guarnacci

The remains of an Etruscan settlement at Roselle

TOP 10 ⭐ Lucca

Lucca is an elegant city of opera and olive oil, Romanesque churches and hidden palace gardens. Its historic centre is contained within massive 16th-century redbrick bastions. The street plan first laid down by the Romans is little altered – in the Middle Ages the ancient amphitheatre was used as a foundation for houses. The composers Boccherini and Puccini were born here, and are celebrated in concerts around the city. More contemporary acts play at the town's renowned annual summer music festival.

Duomo ②

The early 13th-century façade **(right)** stacks Pisan-Romanesque arcades above a portico with Romanesque carvings. Inside are sculptures by 15th-century master Matteo Civitale, Jacopo della Quercia's Tomb of Ilaria, Tintoretto's *Last Supper* (1591) and the revered *Volto Santo di Lucca*, supposedly carved by Nicodemus.

① San Michele in Foro

Built atop the Roman Forum, San Michele's Pisan-Romanesque arcades **(above)** are stacked higher than the Duomo's. Inside are a *Madonna and Child* by Civitale, another by Andrea della Robbia, and a Filippino Lippi *Saints*. Puccini was a chorister here.

③ Tomb of Ilaria

Jacopo della Quercia's masterpiece (1405–7) in the sacristy of the Duomo marries the medieval lying-in-state pose of town boss Paolo Guinigi's young wife (she died at 26) with classical-inspired garlands and cherubs. Jacopo's delicate chisel turned hard marble into soft cushions and captured Ilaria's ethereal beauty.

④ Piazza Anfiteatro

The Roman amphitheatre in Lucca was mined long ago (for building stone), but its oval remained as a base for medieval houses. It is now a quiet piazza **(below)**, with ancient arches still embedded in house walls.

7 Basilica di San Frediano

Treasures here include a Romanesque font and Amico Aspertini's 1508–9 frescoes, the *Miracles of San Frediano*. The façade **(above)** glitters with Byzantine mosaics.

8 The Walls

Chestnuts and umbrella pines shade the gravelly path atop the remarkable ramparts (1544–1650). Locals love to stroll or bicycle here for views into gardens or out over the Apuan Alps.

9 Museo Nazionale di Palazzo Mansi

Riotous Baroque palace interiors serve as the backdrop for Mannerist and Renaissance art by Bronzino, Beccafumi, Correggio, Sodoma and Luca Giordano.

5 Museo Nazionale Villa Guinigi

This 15th-century villa houses a fine archaeology section containing Iron Age, Ligurian and later Etruscan finds, decent Renaissance paintings and wood inlay from the 15th century.

6 Santa Maria Forisportam

Though the Pisan façade is 12th-century, the interior is mostly 17th-century, including two Guercino altarpieces and a *pietre dure* ciborium (inlaid stone vessel).

10 Torre Guinigi

The 14th-century palace of Lucca's ruling family sprouts a 44-m (144-ft) tower **(below)** offering stunning views.

LUCCA'S HISTORY

Villa Guinigi's collections show the region's Stone Age history, but the town was founded by the Romans. Caesar, Pompey and Crassus cemented their First Triumvirate here. St Peter's disciple Paulinus legendarily brought Christianity to Lucca, and it was a waypoint on the Via Francigena pilgrim route. The tough Marquess Mathilda ruled the town during the Lombard period. Succeeded by local lords – except during one 14th-century stint under Pisa – Lucca remained proudly independent of Florence until Napoleon gave the city to his sister Elisa in 1805.

NEED TO KNOW

MAP C2

Visitor information: Piazzale Verdi; 0583 583 150; www.turismo.lucca.it

Duomo: Piazza San Martino; open 10am–6pm Mon–Sat (from noon Sun); adm for tomb

Basilica di San Frediano: open 9:30am–6:30pm daily; adm €3

Torre Guinigi: 0583 48 090; open daily; adm €3

Museo Nazionale di Palazzo Mansi: open noon–7:30pm Tue–Sat (tours on the hour); adm

Museo Nazionale Villa Guinigi: open 9am–7:30pm Tue, Thu, 1st & 3rd Sun of month (from noon Wed, Fri & Sat); adm; combined ticket for museums

- Da Leo *(see p113)* serves delicious soups.
- Piazza Santa Maria has many cycle rental places.

The Top 10
of Everything

Medieval towers rise above
the town of San Gimignano

🔟 Moments in History

Julius Caesar depicted in a fresco at the Pitti Palace

1 Etruscan Civilization

The Etruscans *(see p45)* migrated to Italy around 900 BC, attracted by its mineral wealth. They produced weapons, tools and jewellery to trade with Greece. After a fierce war with Rome in 395 BC, the civilization was eclipsed by Roman rule.

2 Foundation of Florentia

Julius Caesar founded Florence in 59 BC as a settlement for his veteran soldiers. Their encampment was in today's Piazza della Repubblica.

3 Comuni

In the 12th century, Florence became a city-state with self-ruling institutions that grew to conquer other Tuscan cities. The flourishing urban capital gave rise to manufacturing, trade and banking. In the mid-14th century, when Edward III of England defaulted on his debts, the economy grew unstable and many were led to bankruptcy. In 1348, the Black Death killed half the population.

GIOVANNI BOCCACCIO
Statue of Giovanni di Bicci, the first Medici

4 The Medici Rule

During the Renaissance, Tuscany was the leader in intellectual and artistic development. This was due mostly to the patronage of the Medici family. Florence enjoyed a period of peace and prosperity under their rule. In 1569, the Medicis obtained the title 'Grand Dukes' of Tuscany. However, a slow decline began in the 17th century, and their rule ended by 1737.

5 Girolamo Savonarola

After the city was declared a Republic in 1494, the Dominican friar Girolamo Savonarola came to power. He denounced corruption, exploitation of the poor and despotic rule. But in 1498, he was publicly burnt in Piazza della Signoria *(see p83)*. The Republic had to survive 32 years of constant attack after this. In 1530, Pope Clement VII and Charles V, the Holy Roman Emperor combined forces and returned the city to Medici rule.

6 Lorena Rule

The Lorraine family led the region until the unification of Italy, apart from a period of French rule (1799–1814). A key ruler was Peter Leopold (r 1765–1790). His social and economic reforms modernized the Grand Duchy. Notably, he abolished capital punishment in 1786, making Tuscany the first state in the world to do so. Florence remained the capital of Italy until the process of unification (*Risorgimento*) was completed in 1871, and the capital shifted to Rome.

7 Liberation of Florence

During World War II, on 11 August, the partisan brigades of the Resistance liberated Florence just a few days before the arrival of the Allied troops.

8 The Flood

On 4 November 1966, the city was hit by the worst flood in its history, with water reaching the first floor of buildings in the historic centre.

Waterlogging during the flood

9 Rise of Modern Fashion

In 1951, Giovanni Battista Giorgini spearheaded the first international runway show at Villa Torrigiani in the city. Today, the city features designers such as Gucci, Cavalli, Ferragamo and Pucci. Most major boutiques *(see p85)* are located in the commercial district.

10 Green Florence

Florence has developed miles of tramlines, bike paths, cycle lanes and a fleet of electric transport sharing vehicles. Future plans include a 222-acre (90-ha) park, a low-emission zone and a smart control room to digitally manage traffic flow into the city.

TOP 10 MEDICI RULERS

1 Giovanni di Bicci (1360–1429)
Bicci served as head of the Priori government and was a sponsor of Ghiberti's Baptistry commission.

2 Cosimo II Vecchio (1389–1464)
Each time Cosimo the Elder was exiled or imprisoned by rivals, popular sentiment brought him back to power, making him the *de facto* ruler of Florence.

3 Lorenzo the Magnificent (1449–92)
Most beloved of the Medici, Lorenzo was a humanist and patron of the arts. He sponsored Michelangelo's early career.

4 Pope Leo X (Giovanni; 1475–1521)
Lorenzo's son called the shots from Rome, exclaiming "God has risen us to the papacy; let us enjoy it."

5 Pope Clement VII (Giulio; 1478–1534)
Upon becoming pope, his tussle with Emperor Charles V caused him to leave Florence to the young Medicis.

6 Alessandro (1510–37)
Clement VII's illegitimate son inherited the mantle at the age of 19, and soon became a despot. He was murdered by his cousin Lorenzino.

7 Cosimo I (1519–74)
Cosimo became a duke at the age of 17, when the primary Medici line ended.

8 Ferdinando I (1549–1609)
Popular grand duke who gave dowries to girls from poor families, founded hospitals, promoted agriculture and hosted grand parties.

9 Anna Maria (1667–1743)
The last of the main Medici line, she decreed that patrimony never be removed from Florence.

10 Gian Gastone (1671–1737)
The last Medici ruler reversed many of the earlier policies. After him, the grand ducal title passed to the Austrian Lorraines.

Bust of Gian Gastone

🔟 Churches in Florence

1 Duomo
See pp16–17.

2 Santa Maria Novella
MAP L2 ■ Piazza S Maria Novella ■ Opening hours vary, check website ■ Adm ■ www.smn.it

Among the many masterpieces in this beautiful church are *Trinità* (1428) by Masaccio, which had the first use of Renaissance perspective in a painting, the extraordinary, and particularly realistic, *Crucifix* by Giotto, *Cappella Strozzi* frescoes (1486) by Filippino Lippi and the colourful sanctuary frescoes (1485) by Ghirlandaio. The greenish Noah frescoes (1446) are warped perspectives by Paolo Uccello.

3 Santa Croce
Behind the striking marble façade of Florence's "Westminster Abbey" is a Gothic pantheon of cultural heroes that contains the tombs *(see p82)* of well-known figures such as Machiavelli, Michelangelo, Rossini and Galileo (reburied here in

Galileo's tomb in Santa Croce

1737). Giotto frescoed the two chapels sited to the right of the altar.

The interior of San Lorenzo

4 San Lorenzo and the Medici Chapels
MAP M2 ■ Piazza di S Lorenzo ■ Medici Chapel: open 8:15am–6:50pm Mon, Wed–Sat, am only Sun; closed Tue, 1 Jan, 25 Dec ■ Adm

This was the Medici parish church. The family's tombs are decorated by Rosso Fiorentino, Donatello, Bronzino and Filippo Lippi, with architecture by Brunelleschi (interior and Old Sacristy) and Michelangelo (Laurentian Library and New Sacristy). The New Sacristy also contains Michelangelo's roughly finished *Dawn*, *Dusk*, *Day* and *Night*.

5 Santo Spirito
MAP L5 ■ Piazza S Spirito ■ Open 10am–1pm & 3–6pm Mon–Sat, 11:30am–1:30pm & 3–6pm Sun & hols; closed Wed

The proportions of Brunelleschi's Renaissance masterpiece are picked out in clean lines of *pietra serena* stone against white plaster. See the altarpieces by Filippino Lippi (*Madonna and Child with Saints*, 1466) and Verrocchio (*St Monica and Augustinian Nuns*).

The church of San Miniato al Monte

provided the Mannerist façade, while the artist Ghirlandaio frescoed the Cappella Sasetti with the *Life of St Francis* set in 15th-century Florence.

9 Orsanmichele

MAP M4 ▪ Via dell'Arte della Lana ▪ Open 10am–6pm Tue & Sat

This granary-turned-church, once used by the city's trade guilds, is ringed with statues by Donatello, Ghiberti and Verrocchio (all copies; the originals are in the museum upstairs). Orcagna designed the tabernacle to resemble a cathedral and it contains *Madonna and Child with Angels*, a 1348 work by Daddi.

6 San Miniato al Monte

MAP Q6 ▪ Via Monte alle Croci ▪ Open 9:30am–1pm & 3–7pm Mon–Sat, 8:15am–7pm Sun

Perched high above the city, this is Florence's only Romanesque church. The doors of Michelozzo's taber-nacle were painted by Agnolo Gaddi (1394–6), one of the last Florentine artists stylistically descended from Giotto.

7 Santa Maria del Carmine

MAP K4 ▪ Piazza del Carmine ▪ Open 10am–5pm Mon, Fri–Sat (from 1pm Sun & hols) ▪ Adm for Brancacci Chapel; advance booking for church (0552 768 224)

Masolino started the Brancacci Chapel's frescoes of St Peter's life in 1424. Another of his works, *Adam and Eve*, is rather sweet compared to the powerful *Expulsion from the Garden* by his successor, Masaccio. Filippino Lippi completed the cycle in 1485.

10 Santissima Annunziata

MAP P1 ▪ Piazza SS Annunziata ▪ Open 7:30am–12:30pm & 4–6:30pm daily

The Michelozzo-designed entry cloister was frescoed by Mannerists Andrea del Sarto, Rosso and Pontormo. The octagonal Baroque tribune is decorated with Perugino's *Madonna and Saints* and Bronzino's *Resurrection*. In the back chapel, sculptures by Giambologna himself adorn his tomb.

Statue of St George, Orsanmichele

8 Santa Trinita

MAP L4 ▪ Piazza S Trinita ▪ Open 8am–noon & 4–6pm Mon–Sat, 4–6pm Sun & hols

Florentine artist and architect Buontalenti

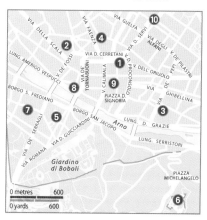

0 metres 600
0 yards 600

🔟 Churches outside Florence

Detail of the portal at Massa Marittima's Duomo

1 Siena's Duomo
The Duomo in Siena (see pp30–31) is a striped Romanesque-Gothic pile, richly decorated by Giovanni Pisano, Michelangelo, Pinturicchio, Donatello, Beccafumi and Bernini.

2 San Gimignano's Collegiata
MAP D3 ▪ Piazza del Duomo ▪ Open Apr–Oct: 10am–7:30pm Mon–Fri, 10am–5:30pm Sat, 12:30–7:30pm Sun; Nov–Mar: 10am–5pm Mon–Sat, 12:30–5pm Sun ▪ Closed during religious services; 1 & 15–31 Jan, 12 Mar, 15–30 Nov, 25 Dec ▪ Adm

The medieval Manhattan's main church (see p24) features an interior covered with 14th- and 15th-century frescoes, including a cycle by the Italian painter Ghirlandaio.

3 Pisa's Duomo
Only a few elements (see p26), such as the Pisan-Romanesque exterior and Cimabue's apse mosaic of 1302, survived a 1595 fire. However, the late Renaissance/early Baroque refurbishment was stylish, and local legend holds the swinging of the nave's large bronze lamp inspired Galileo's Law of Pendulums.

4 Lucca's Duomo
San Martino (see p46) is a masterpiece of Romanesque stacked open arcades, stuffed with sculpture from Gothic reliefs to works by two great 15th-century talents, local Matteo Civitale and Sienese Jacopo della Quercia.

5 Massa Marittima's Duomo
MAP D4/5 ▪ Piazza Garibaldi ▪ Open 9am–noon & 3–5pm daily (summer: until 7pm)

A cathedral with a split personality, Massa Marittima's Duomo features Romanesque arcading which is topped by Gothic pinnacles and a bell tower. It houses some wonderfully idiosyncratic sculpture: three takes on the life of local patron San Cerbone as well as some lovely pre-Romanesque carvings.

6 Sant'Antimo
Although this isolated Cistercian abbey (see p121) was founded by Charlemagne, the present building dates only from 1118. Inside visitors will find several beautifully carved column capitals. Monks pray in chant five times daily; if asked, they can show you the sacristy's earthy frescoes.

The abbey of Sant'Antimo

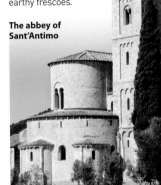

7 Arezzo's San Francesco

A 15-year restoration of the choir's *Legend of the True Cross* (1448–66), the greatest fresco cycle by Piero della Francesca, has revived the vitality and vibrancy of this arresting 14th-century church *(see p103)*.

8 Pienza's Duomo

Behind the Classical façade of the Duomo is a reinterpreted German Gothic hall church building *(see p121)* which is a part of a collection of structures that, as a group, form a UNESCO World Heritage Site. Dating from the 15th century, these struc-tures are a direct result of Piccolomini Pope Pius II's interference in Rossellino's initial plan to build the perfect Renaissance town.

9 Pistoia's Duomo

Andrea della Robbia's enamelled terracotta entrance accents the zebra stripes of the Romanesque exterior of the Duomo in Pistoia *(see p89)*. The Altar of St Jacopo (1287–1456) contains

St Nicholas at Pienza's Duomo

some of the finest silversmithing in Italy. Ask the custodian to show you Verrocchio's striking 1485 *Madonna di Piazza*.

10 Prato's Duomo

Some of the finest art in all of Prato can be found decorating the Duomo *(see p89)*. Michelozzo's out-side pulpit ensures that crowds in the piazza are able to see the bishop display the Virgin's girdle *(see p33)*. Fra Filippo Lippi's graceful frescoes in the choir are considered his most important works and include the famous scene of Salomé holding the head of John the Baptist on a platter at Herod's banquet.

The Feast of Herod by Fra Filippo Lippi at Prato's Duomo

📟 Museums

1 Florence's Uffizi
Botticelli's *Birth of Venus*, Leonardo's *Annunciation* and Michelangelo's *Tondo Doni* are just three of the masterpieces that make this *(see pp12–15)* the top sight in all of Tuscany.

2 Florence's Pitti Palace
The Galleria Palatina features Raphael Madonnas and Titian beauties alongside works by Andrea del Sarto, Perugino, Signorelli, Rubens and Caravaggio. Palatial décor is the setting for collections *(see pp18–21)* of costumes, silverware and carriages.

3 Siena's Museo Civico
A battlemented medieval town hall *(see p36)* with the best Gothic painting in Siena, including Lorenzetti's incomparable *Allegory of Good and Bad Government*.

4 Florence's Bargello
Italy's top sculpture gallery *(see p82)* is set in a former town hall and prison dating to 1255, and takes its name from the office of the city's police chief or *bargello* that was once based here. The gallery contains the world's best collection of Donatellos. It also holds sculptures by Cellini, Giambologna and Michelangelo.

5 Cortona's Museo dell'Accademia Etrusca
MAP F4 ▪ Piazza Signorelli ▪ Open 10am–7pm daily (Nov–Mar: 10am–1pm & 2–5pm Tue–Sun) ▪ Adm

This collection *(see p44)* preserves Etruscan finds as well as Renaissance and Baroque paintings, plus a few Egyptian artifacts, decorative arts and paintings by the Futurist artist Gino Severini who lived locally. Ginori Temple and the library are temporarily closed.

A gallery at the Accademia, Florence

6 Florence's Galleria dell'Accademia
Visitors come for Michelangelo's *David*, then stay for his *Slaves*, carved for the tomb of Julius II, and art by Botticelli, Lorenzo di Credi, Orcagna, Perugino and del Sarto. The plaster casts crowding one long room hint that this is still a fine arts academy *(see p81)*. The statues' black "pimples" are reference points to help students copy the works.

7 Sansepolcro's Museo Civico
Piero della Francesca's hometown *(see p103)* has retained some of his greatest, most psychologically penetrating works, alongside works by Signorelli and natives Santi di Tito and Raffaellino del Colle. Works housed in the museum include *Madonna della Misericordia* (1445–62), *San Giuliano* (1458) and the *Resurrection* (1463), called "the best picture in the world" by Aldous Huxley in a 1925 essay.

Bronze Etruscan chandelier in Cortona's museum

8 Florence's Museo Galileo

MAP N5 ▪ Piazza dei Giudici 1 ▪ Open 9:30am–6pm Wed–Mon (until 1pm Tue) ▪ Adm

The instruments displayed here are often as beautiful as they are scientifically significant. Exhibits include a mechanical "calculator" made of engraved disks, a perpetual motion machine and the telescopes with which Galileo discovered the moons of Jupiter.

9 Siena's Pinacoteca Nazionale

Set in a 14th-century palazzo *(see p95)*, this comprehensive survey of Sienese painting is Tuscany's best. The gallery houses Bartolo di Fredi's *Adoration of the Magi* (though the masterpieces of the school are housed elsewhere).

Adoration of the Magi by di Fredi

10 Volterra's Museo Etrusco Guarnacci

MAP D4 ▪ Via Don Minzoni 15 ▪ Open 9am–7pm daily (Nov–Mar: 10am–4:30pm) ▪ Adm

One of Tuscany's top Etruscan museums *(see p44)*, with over 600 marble and alabaster funerary urns carved with myths or metaphors for the afterlife, a terracotta sarcophagus lid of an elderly couple, and small bronzes including the elongated boyish figure, *Shade of the Evening*.

TOP 10 ARTISTIC STYLES

Macchiaioli-style work by Abbati

1 Macchiaioli
Tuscan cousin of Impressionism (late 19th century).

2 Byzantine
Conservative, static, stylized in Eastern iconographic tradition of the 9th–13th centuries AD. Almond faces, large eyes, robes pleated in gold cross-hatching.

3 Gothic
More expressive, colourful and realistic than Byzantine. Flowing lines and dramatic gestures (13th–14th centuries).

4 Renaissance
Tuscany's greatest contribution to art history. In their elegant compositions, the 15th- and 16th-century Florentine artists developed a more naturalistic style as well as complex techniques such as perspective.

5 Mannerism
Late Renaissance, 16th-century offshoot based on Michelangelo's rich colour palette and twisting poses.

6 Baroque
Similar to Mannerism, but using strong contrasts of light and shade to achieve high drama (16th–17th centuries).

7 Rococo
Baroque gone chaotic, effusive and overwrought (18th century).

8 Neo-Classical
Based on classical models and mythological themes (19th century).

9 Etruscan
Heavily influenced by Greek art, the style is seen in large statues, funerary urns and bronze votives from the 8th to the 4th centuries BC.

10 Liberty
Italian 20th-century Art Nouveau, seen mostly on façades and shop signs.

🔟 Tuscan Masterpieces

1 David
Florence

At the age of 26, Michelangelo took on a huge slab of marble, nicknamed "the Giant" by the sculptors of the day, and turned it into *David* (1501–4), an intense young man contemplating his task as a proper Renaissance humanist would. Intended for Florence's Duomo, it first stood in front of the Palazzo Vecchio. Damaged during an anti-Medici riot, it was eventually wheeled to the Galleria dell'Accademia *(see p81)* for safekeeping.

2 Birth of Venus
Florence

Housed in the Uffizi *(see p12)*, Botticelli's beauty strikes a classical, modest pose, covering her nakedness with her hands while an *Ora* (handmaiden) rushes to clothe her and the west wind, Zephyr, blows her gracefully to shore in a swirl of pink roses (c.1484–6).

Michelangelo's David

3 Rosso Fiorentino's Deposition
Volterra

The garish colours and twisted poses are the classic hallmarks of Florentine Mannerism, and this is one of its masterpieces. Its shockingly modern take on a traditional subject feels much more recent than 1521. It is housed in the Pinacoteca *(see p115)*.

4 Gates of Paradise
Florence

It took Ghiberti years (1425–52) to complete ten gilded bronze panels of Old Testament scenes on the Baptistry's *(see p16)* east doors (now copies; originals in the Museo dell'Opera).

5 Trinità
Florence

Masaccio's *Trinità*, set in Santa Maria Novella *(see p52)*, was painted in 1428. It is the first painting to use the mathematical single point perspective. The triangular composition of the work draws lines from two kneeling donors straight through the halos of Mary and St John to God the Father.

6 Duccio's Maestà
Siena

An altarpiece composed of several individual paintings, this was the first undisputed masterpiece of the Sienese School. It was paraded through the streets before its installation, and

Duccio di Buoninsegna's *Maestà* depicting an enthroned Madonna and Child

painting a *Maestà* became a rite of passage for artists. It is set in Museo dell'Opera Metropolitana *(see p32)*.

7 Giovanni Pisano's Pulpit
Pistoia

The Pisanos (father and son) carved four stone pulpits, in Pisa, Siena and Pistoia. Located in Sant'Andrea *(see p89)*, Giovanni's hexagonal 1301 pulpit depicts, in gory Gothic detail, biblical tales such as the "Last Judgement".

8 Giotto's Maestà
Florence

On display at the Uffizi, Giotto's masterful work (1310) broke conventions by dressing the Virgin in normal clothes rather than stylized robes, with the Child perched on an actual lap rather than hovering.

9 Allegory of Good and Bad Government
Siena

Located in Museo Civico *(see p34)*, Ambrogio Lorenzetti's 1338 fresco wraps around the medieval ruling Council of Nine's chambers. Ruled by figures of Good Government, medieval Siena prospers, while ruled by Bad Government, it crumbles.

Lorenzetti's *Allegory of Government*

10 Resurrection of Christ
Sansepolcro

Piero della Francesca's muscled, heavy-lidded Jesus rises from his sarcophagus, bringing the dreary, dead landscape flowers to life (1463). The sleeping Roman soldier slumped in brown armour is said to be a self-portrait. The painting can be viewed at the Museo Civico *(see p103)*.

TOP 10 TUSCAN ARTISTS

Lithograph of Giotto di Bondone

1 Giotto (1266–1337)
Giotto took painting from its static, Byzantine style and set it on the road to the Renaissance.

2 Simone Martini (1284–1344)
Martini took a medieval eye for iconography and married it to a vibrant palette and intense drama.

3 Donatello (1386–1466)
The first Renaissance sculptor worked out perspective before the painters, and cast the first equestrian statue and first freestanding nude since antiquity.

4 Fra Angelico (1395–1455)
Manuscript illumination informed his art, but Angelico's work is based on the ideas of naturalism and perspective.

5 Masaccio (1401–28)
Masaccio imbued Renaissance painting with an unflinching naturalism and perfected single point perspective.

6 Piero della Francesca (1416–92)
A visionary whose compositions have an ethereal spirituality, well-modelled figures and a mastery of perspective.

7 Botticelli (1444–1510)
The master of grand mythological scenes is said to have tossed his own "blasphemous" works upon the Bonfire of the Vanities *(see p82)*.

8 Leonardo da Vinci (1452–1519)
The ultimate Renaissance Man: a painter, proto-scientist and inventor, with a penchant for experimentation.

9 Michelangelo (1475–1564)
Famously irascible, he was a sculptor of genius by his early 20s.

10 Plautilla Nelli (1524–1588)
A Florence native, Nelli was a nun as well as a self-taught painter. She is considered one of the city's first female Renaissance artists.

🔟 Hill Towns

Town hall, Cortona

② Siena
MAP E4

Siena may have grown to small city size (see pp30–37), but it retains a homey, hill-town atmosphere (see pp94–9). Its travertine-accented brick palaces, stone towers and fabulously decorated churches are strung along three high ridges at the south end of the Chianti hills.

③ Volterra
MAP D4

The world's greatest alabaster craftsmen inhabit the loftiest hill town in Tuscany, whose stony medieval streets rise a cloud-scraping 555 m (1,820 ft) above the valley. This was one of the key cities in the Etruscan Dodecapolis confederation (see pp44–5). The museum (see p57) is filled with finds unearthed as the erosion that is affecting one end of town slowly exposes ancient tombs.

① Cortona
MAP F4

This Etruscan settlement (see pp42–5) above the Chiana Valley is a trove of ancient tombs and Renaissance art. Stony buildings, steep streets and interlocked *piazze* characterize the centre. The upper town has the Sanctuary of St Margaret, the 16th-century Medici fortress and little-known lookouts.

Pienza *pecorino*

④ Pienza
MAP F4

Italy's only perfectly planned, Pienza Renaissance town centre (see p121) was commissioned from Rossellino by Pope Pius II in the 15th century. The perimeter street offers views over the rumpled green, sheep-dotted landscape. The town's shops specialize in Tuscan wines, honey and the best *pecorino* sheep's milk cheese in all of Italy.

Montepulciano, with Tempio di San Biagio church in the foreground

7 Montalcino
MAP E4

Montalcino *(see p121)* stands proudly high above the valley; this was Siena's last ally against Florentine rule. The hilltop eyrie is dominated by the shell of a 14th-century fortress with fantastic views, and is now a place where you can sample Montalcino's Brunello wine *(see pp70–71)*, the region's most robust red.

8 Massa Marittima
MAP D4/5

The Old Town *(see p115)* centres on a triangular piazza with the Duomo and the crenellated mayor's palazzo. The upper New Town was founded in the 14th century by the conquering Sienese, whose fortress now offers visitors sweeping hill views. The Museum of Sacred Art in the museum complex of San Pietro all'Orto holds Ambrogio Lorenzetti's *Maestà*.

The clifftop town of Pitigliano

5 San Gimignano
MAP D3

This medieval Manhattan – a UNESCO World Heritage Site and the epitome of the perfect Italian hill town – features 14 stone towers of varying heights (the tallest 54 m/177 ft) that seem to sprout from the terracotta roof tiles. The town *(see p115)* is surrounded by patchwork fields and vineyards that produce Tuscany's best DOCG white wine *(see pp24–5)*.

6 Montepulciano
MAP F4

From the Medici city gate to the hilltop Piazza Grande with its cren-ellated Michelozzo-designed Palazzo Comunale and brick-façaded Duomo, the main street passes *palazzi*, 19th-century cafés and wine shops where the samples of grappa and Vino Nobile *(see pp70–71)* flow freely. You can also visit the cellars beneath the town *(see p121)*.

9 Pitigliano
MAP F6

In the heart of the Alta Maremma, surrounded by valleys full of old tombs, Pitigliano *(see p127)* is home to a his-torically important Jewish community. It is built upon an outcrop of tufa rock. In fact, it is difficult to tell where the cliff sides end – pockmarked as they are with cellar windows – and the walls of the houses and castle begin.

10 Fiesole
MAP E2

Roman Florentia was built to compete with this hilltop town *(see p89)*. Fiesole has archaeology and art museums, a Roman theatre, cool summertime breezes and views across to Florence.

🔟 Villas and Gardens

1 Villa Poggio a Caiano

Giuliano da Sangallo restructured this greatest of Medici villas (see p90) in 1480 for Lorenzo the Magnificent. Until this point, country houses were fortified, with rooms facing an inner courtyard. Sangallo's design was revolutionary, with rooms overlooking the countryside and a central hall with frescoes. The ballroom is a pinnacle of Mannerist painting by Pontormo, Andrea del Sarto, Filippino Lippi and Alessandro Allori. Francesco I and his second wife Bianca Cappello died here in 1587, apparently poisoned.

2 Villa Torrigiani

MAP D2 ▪ Via Gomberaio 3, Camigliano, Capannori ▪ 0583 928 041 ▪ Open Nov–May: 10am–1pm & 3–5pm daily (summer: until 6:30 pm)

Two magnificent wings of cypress trees announce this Renaissance villa and gardens. Rebuilt to form a majestic estate in the first half of the 17th century by the Marquis Nicolao Santini the garden was inspired by the Palace of Versailles and decorated with flowered parterres, caves and a pool to reflect the villa's façade.

3 Villa Vignamaggio

MAP E3 ▪ Vignamaggio, Greve ▪ 0558 546 653 ▪ Open daily ▪ Adm ▪ www.vignamaggio.com

The villa's wines were, in 1404, the first to be called "Chianti" (see p40). This is also where the real Mona Lisa was born (1479) and where Kenneth Branagh's *Much Ado about Nothing* (1993) was filmed. Guided tours offer wine samples; a full tour includes lunch in the *enoteca*.

Villa Poggio a Caiano

Appennino sculpture, Villa Demido⊠

(4) Villa Demidoff

Buontalenti laid out the vast Pratolino park *(see p90)* for Francesco I de' Medici (1568–81). It was created for Bianca Cappello, Francesco's mistress, and served as a setting for their wedding in 1579. The waterworks have long fallen into disrepair (the villa was demolished in 1824), but what remains is still spectacular, especially the figure of Appennino rising out of a lily pond.

(5) Villa di Artimino "La Ferdinanda"

MAP D2 ■ Artimino, Carmignano ■ 055 875 141 ■ House: open by appointment

This 16th-century Buontalenti villa was built for Ferdinando I, most likely as a winter hunting lodge. Visitors can dine or spend the night here or pop into the wellness centre on the premises.

(6) Villa di Castello

MAP E2 ■ Via di Castello 44, Sesto Fiorentino ■ 055 452 691 ■ Opening hours vary, call ahead to check ■ Adm

Cosimo I had Tribolo lay out the marvellous gardens in 1541, a combination of clipped hedges, ponds, ilex woods and statuary. The villa hosts the prestigious Accademia della Crusca, an Italian linguistics society.

(7) Villa Reale di Marlia

MAP D2 ■ Marlia, Capannori ■ 0583 30 009 ■ Open Mar–Oct: 10am–6pm daily ■ Closed Nov–Feb ■ Adm

This 16th-century villa was radically altered by Elisa Baciocchi to suit her 19th-century Napoleonic tastes. Only the 17th-century gardens are open to visitors.

(8) Villa Garzoni

MAP D2 ■ Collodi ■ Open 9am–sunset daily (Mar–Oct: from 10am) ■ Adm ■ www.pinocchio.it

The villa (1633–52) is currently closed to the public, but the Renaissance and Baroque garden, set into a steep hillside, is open to visitors.

The gardens of Villa Mansi

(9) Villa Mansi

MAP D2 ■ Segromigno in Monte ■ 0583 920 234 ■ Open Apr–Oct: 2–6pm daily ■ Closed Sat & Sun ■ Adm

This impressive 16th-century villa is studded with a selection of statues and contains mythological frescoes painted in the late 18th century. Juvarra's Baroque gardens survive to the west side of the villa; the rest were landscaped in English style in the 19th century.

(10) Villa Medicea di Cerreto Guidi

This beautiful villa *(see p90)*, set close to the medieval capital of the Mugello region, was built in the mid-1500s as a hunting lodge for the Medici family. Today it houses the incredible Hunting Museum and an art gallery.

⏏10 **Spas and Resorts**

Colonnaded spa pool at Montecatini Terme

① **Montecatini Terme**
The best place *(see p110)* in Italy for grandiose, Liberty-style thermal establishments, this town has a lot to offer visitors. Drink Terme Tettuccio's waters for your digestive system, wallow in Terme Leopoldine's mud for your skin. Also take the funicular to the medieval hill town of Montecatini Alto.

② **Viareggio**
MAP C2

Southernmost Riviera-style resort *(see p109)* on the coast, Viareggio is a mix of grand old buildings and simple tourist hotels. The promenade is lined with restaurants and shops on one side, and a crowded but sandy beach on the other (all stretches are privately run; you need to pay for a chair and umbrella). Not the cleanest water, but the calm sea and sandy beach are good for children.

③ **Cascate del Mulino, Saturnia**
MAP E6

After Saturnia's sulphur-laden hot spring bursts out of the ground, it rushes over the Cascate del Mulino *(see p128)*, a long slope of open-air whirlpools that form a staircase of waterfalls and small azure pools. There, you can lie back in the warm, bubbly waters and relax for free.

④ **Saturnia Spa**
An elegant four-star spa *(see p128)*, the Hotel Terme di Saturnia is built around the town's sulphur spring, whose warm waters and mineral-rich mud have long been thought to benefit the skin and respiratory system. A fitness centre is attached to the hotel, and there are also opportunities for horse riding.

⑤ Monsummano Terme

Located near Montecatini Terme, this natural sauna *(see p110)* is formed from a series of subterranean caves that lie above a sulphurous underground lake, filled with hot mineral-laden vapours.

⑥ Elba
MAP C5

Italy's third largest island *(see p127)* offers Tuscany's best all-round coastal holiday – sandy beaches, watersports, fishing villages, resorts and vineyards. Sightseeing takes in forts, museums and mine tours devoted to the island's mineralogical wealth (discovered by the Etruscans, the iron of Elba armed the legions of Rome). There are also two villas left from the 11 months Napoleon lived here in exile.

⑦ Punta Ala
MAP D5

This is little more than a modern yacht marina backed by some classy hotels. Nearby, there is horse riding on offer and one of Tuscany's toughest, and prettiest, golf courses amid pine groves sloping down to the sea.

⑧ Chianciano Terme
MAP F4 ■ www.chianciano terme.com

It is fortunate that the spa waters of Acqua Santa clean the liver, for the historic spa town of Chianciano lies at the end of a wine road from Montalcino past the Val d'Orcia and Montepulciano. This group of thermal spas – with waters and mud packs

Wisteria garden, Chianciano Terme

to invigorate the body – is linked to the hill town of Chianciano Alto by a long string of hotels.

⑨ Monte Argentario
MAP E6

This mountainous peninsula *(see p127)* is covered in ilex and olives, and rimmed with beaches. The trendier of its two towns is southerly Porto Ercole, where Caravaggio died. It retains a fishing village air, while Porto Santo Stefano is a slightly larger resort town and the main fishing port.

⑩ Forte dei Marmi
MAP C2

One of the string of impeccable beaches along the northern Versilia, Forte dei Marmi *(see p111)* is built around a 15th-century marble port. It stands out for its fine sands, grand ducal fort (1788) and the villas of minor nobility and the well-to-do hidden amid the pines.

A beach at Forte dei Marmi

🔟 Tuscany for Children

The Ildebranda Tomb at the Etruscan necropolis in Sovana

1 Exploring Tombs

Crawling through the ancient tunnels and tombs left by the Etruscans makes for a slightly spooky Indiana Jones-style adventure. The best are in the Maremma around Sorano (see p129), Sovana (see p128) and Pitigliano (see p127), and near Chiusi (see p122).

2 Climbing the Towers and Domes

From the Duomo's dome in Florence to countless bell towers across the region, Tuscany offers youngsters dozens of fun scrambles up to dramatic lookout points, many reached only via tight, evocatively medieval sets of stairs.

3 Life at Court

https://tickets museums.comune.fi.it/ 13_life-at-court/

Palazzo Vecchio's (see p83) tour takes kids through a secret door into the private chambers of the Medici and their 11 children. Dress up in ducal costumes and get a glimpse into noble life in the Middle Ages.

Puppet, Pinocchio Park

4 Saturnia Hot Springs

Sit back and relax in a warm sulphur pool (see p66) while your offspring splash and make Italian friends in this open-air slice of paradise (see p128). But keep little ones away from the upper parts of the stream where the current is very strong.

5 Biking Lucca's Walls

Cycle around the top of Lucca's massive 16th-century ramparts shaded by trees, and peek down into elaborate gardens.

6 Pinocchio Park, Collodi

MAP D2 ■ Off the S435 outside Collodi ■ Opening hours vary, check website ■ Adm ■ www.pinocchio.it/ en/orari-parco

The hometown of *Pinocchio* author Carlo "Collodi" Lorenzini has a small themed park.

7 San Gimignano

The Town of Towers is an imposing sight: a medieval fairytale city (see pp24–5) full of towers to climb, alleys to explore and a half-ruined fortress to clamber about. The town is also home to the Museum of Torture, which appeals to children and adults alike.

8 Ludoteca, Florence
MAP J1 ■ Marcondirondero: Via della Carra 4 ■ 055 334 046 ■ Open 4–7pm Mon–Fri

Best suited to toddlers and small children, this city-run service offers two large colourful rooms full of toys. Registration is free but children must be accompanied by an adult.

9 Museo Stibbert, Florence
MAP E3 ■ Via F Stibbert 26 ■ 055 475 520 ■ Open 10am–2pm Mon–Wed, 10am–6pm Fri–Sun ■ Closed Thu ■ Adm ■ www.museostibbert.it

This quirky private museum *(see p84)* of armour was established by art collector Frederick Stibbert. The 16th-century Florentine weaponry is arranged as an army marching through the largest room.

Exhibits at the Museo Stibbert

10 Giardino dei Tarocchi
MAP E6 ■ Garavicchio di Capalbio ■ 0564 895 122 ■ Open Apr–mid-Oct: 2:30–7:30pm daily ■ Adm

This odd sculpture garden is filled with giant Tarot card images mosaicked with Gaudíesque coloured tile chips. French-American artist Niki de Saint Phalle, who created the sculptures, sadly passed away in 2002.

TOP 10 TIPS FOR FAMILIES

Sightseeing at Florence's Duomo

1 Sightseeing Discounts
Ridotto tickets are for students and under-18s. Admission may be free for those under the ages of 6, 12 or even 18 (especially for EU citizens).

2 Try Picnicking
Picnicking is great fun and saves money. Kids can eat what they want, and take a break from places where they have to be on their best behaviour.

3 Order Half-Portions
A *mezza porzione* for smaller appetites costs less.

4 Share a Room
An extra bed costs at most 35 per cent more; cots and baby cribs even less.

5 Make a Base
Stay in one hotel or apartment and make day-trips. Changing hotels is a time-consuming hassle, and weekly rates are cheaper.

6 Train Discounts
Both Italo and the state railway offer discounts for families travelling together. You will save even more if you book long-distance rail travel three months in advance.

7 Rent a Car
One car is usually cheaper than four sets of train tickets.

8 Gelato Breaks
Don't overpack your itinerary. Take time to enjoy the ice cream instead.

9 Use Rest Wisely
Sightseeing is exhausting. Do as the Italians do and nap after lunch.

10 Expect to be Welcomed
Italy is a multigenerational culture, accustomed to welcoming travellers. Attempting a little Italian is a great icebreaker with locals.

TOP 10 Wine Houses

1 Antinori (Chianti)
The Antinori Marquises have been making wine since 1385, producing more than 15 million bottles annually of some of Italy's most highly ranked and consistently lauded wines. You can sample their *vini* at Florence's Cantinetta Antinori *(see p87)*.

2 Avignonesi (Montepulciano)
MAP F4 ▪ Via Colonica 1, Valiano di Montepulciano
▪ www.avignonesi.it
The Falvo brothers were key in reviving the quality and raising the status of Vino Nobile in the 1990s. The huge estate also produces vintages made with Merlot and Cabernet, and one of Tuscany's finest Vin Santos. A classy show-room/free tasting bar is in Montepulciano.

3 Castello di Brolio (Chianti)
The estate *(see p40)* that invented modern Chianti Classico is back in the Ricasoli family after years under Seagram's, and the wines have improved vastly. The "Iron Baron" Bettino Ricasoli, Italy's second prime minister, perfected the formula here in the 19th century.

Bottle of Antinori wine

4 Banfi (Montalcino)
MAP E4 ▪ Call ahead for guided tours (0577 840 111)
▪ www.banfi.it
A massive American-owned estate founded in 1978, Banfi produces scientifically perfect wines and a massive Brunello *riserva*. There's a huge shop and *enoteca* and a small glass and wine museum.

5 Monsanto (Chianti)
Full-bodied wines from the estate *(see p40)* that was the first, in 1968, to make a single *cru* Chianti and a 100 per cent Sangiovese Chianti.

6 Poggio Antico (Montalcino)
MAP E4 ▪ 0577 848 044 ▪ www.poggioantico.com
One of the least pretentious major Montalcino vineyards, this produces an award-winning velvety Brunello. They offer guided cellar tours.

7 Gattavecchi (Montepulciano)
MAP F4 ▪ Via di Collazzi 74
▪ www.gattavecchi.it
Top-rank Vino Nobile producer with grotto-like cellars that burrow under the adjacent church. Riserva dei Padri Serviti is their top wine.

Vineyards at the historic Castello di Brolio estate

La Cucina di Lilian offers lunchtime tasting menus pairing local produce with Gattavecchi wines and olive oil.

8 Marchesi de' Frescobaldi (Chianti Rufina/Montalcino)

MAP E4 ■ www.frescobaldi.it

The Frescobaldi Marquises, the largest private winemaking concern in Tuscany, have been viticulturalists for 30 generations (England's Henry VIII kept some stock on hand). They were one of the first to experiment with non-native grapes (Cabernet Sauvignon, Chardonnay, Merlot, Pinots). You can visit several estates.

Barrels at Marchesi de' Frescobaldi

9 Fonterutoli (Chianti)

Highly regarded estate (see p40) in the Mazzei family since 1435, centred around a medieval village with a laid-back bar (in the osteria) for tippling. Vintages of the Chianti, Siepi and Brancaia have won the top Italian rankings.

10 Tenuta di Capezzana (Carmignano)

MAP D2 ■ Direct sales 10am–6pm Mon–Sat ■ www.capezzana.it

A vineyard since 804, Capezzana single-handedly created the Carmignano DOC by adding 15 per cent Cabernet to the otherwise Sangiovese mix. They also make a rosé version called Vin Ruspo. Book ahead for tastings, or to sign up for the on-site cookery school.

TOP 10 TUSCAN WINE STYLES

Bottles of Chianti wine

1 Chianti Classico and Chianti Classico Gran Selezione
Italy's most famous reds, these are the highest quality Chiantis. Made in a region at whose heart is the original area established by Cosimo III's edict.

2 Brunello di Montalcino
One of Italy's most powerful, complex reds, Brunello is created using only the Sangiovese Grosso varietal – the wine was perfected accidentally when a blight killed all but this grape.

3 Vino Nobile di Montepulciano
Less complex, but more versatile, than Brunello. This Chianti-like blend is dominated by the Prugnolo varietal.

4 Vernaccia di San Gimignano
Tuscany's only white DOCG, a dry to semisweet pale honey elixir.

5 Sassicaia di Bolgheri
Complex, long-lived and very pricey Cabernet Sauvignon.

6 Tignanello
Antinori's complex, beefy wine made with 80 per cent Sangiovese, 15 per cent Cabernet Sauvignon and 5 per cent Cabernet Franc.

7 Chianti Rufina
This is a structured, Sangiovese-based wine from the best-known of the Chianti subzones.

8 Carmignano
One of the world's oldest official wine areas (1716), near Prato. DOCG Chianti blend with Cabernet.

9 Morellino di Scansano
Maremma's big DOC red, 85–100 per cent Morellino (Sangiovese).

10 Vin Santo
Sweet, golden dessert wine made from raisined grapes. Aged in oak barrels.

🔟 Restaurants

Exterior of Antica Locanda di Sesto

1 Antica Locanda di Sesto, near Lucca

There's been an inn here on the banks of the River Serchio between Lucca and the Garfagnana since the 1300s. Family-run for decades, the current incarnation *(see p113)* is steeped in the cooking traditions of this mountainous corner of Tuscany. Several ingredients, including extra-virgin olive oil, are sourced fresh from the family farm. Grilled meat is a house speciality.

2 L'Antica Scuderia, Badia a Passignano

Set amid a sea of vines beside an 11th-century abbey, this *(see p93)* has one of Tuscany's prettiest out-door terraces. The food is equally elegant, a refined take on Tuscan classics such as pappa al pomodoro (a delicious thick tomato soup) and tagliata (a dressed sliced steak). Black truffles feature liberally on the menu.

3 Il Romito, Livorno

Spectacularly perched on a clifftop overlooking the sea, this res-taurant's location *(see p113)* is truly superb. The menu features excellent seafood dishes. Visitors can enjoy a drink at the bar before going on to dine on the spacious terrace. Also on the terrace is a good pizzeria.

4 La Buca di Sant'Antonio, Lucca

This restaurant has been serving the best food in Lucca since 1782. Here *(see p113)* diners will find a series of rooms hung with old kitchen imple-ments and musical instruments. You will experience the friendliest profes-sional welcome of any restaurant in Tuscany, and great Lucchese cooking.

5 Dorandò, San Gimignano

This elegant, stone-walled restaurant *(see p119)* keeps tradi-tional Sangimignanese recipes alive, resurrecting superbly prepared, tasty dishes from the Middle Ages and Renaissance. They even claim that some of their dishes date back to the Etruscan era. The menu explains every dish in detail.

6 Konnubio, Florence

Florence's San Lorenzo neighbourhood is experiencing a mini-renaissance, and this relaxed and friendly restaurant *(see p87)* is certainly worth a visit. The menu is an unusual mix of traditional Tuscan and vegan dishes, occa-sionally on the same plate (seitan with Tuscan spices, for example). The enclosed courtyard setting and subtle lighting gives it a romantic ambience after dark.

Vegan soybean and sprout soup

The lovely rural trattoria La Cantinetta di Rignana

7 La Cantinetta di Rignana, near Greve in Chianti

This establishment *(see p93)* is set amid vineyards, far from anywhere along winding dirt roads – a complete countryside trattoria experience. Curing meats hang in the doorway, and Madonna and Child icons and copper pots pepper the walls. The homemade pastas and grilled meats are delicious. There is also a glassed-in veranda for summertime dining.

8 La Botte Piena, near Montefollonico

Mighty stone-and-brick walls and an oak-beamed ceiling give this place *(see p125)* a rustic vibe. The food follows centuries-old traditions of the Sienese countryside, with the likes of hand-rolled *pici* pasta, *pecorino* cheese and *Cinta Senese* pork. The wine list is long and expertly sourced, and covers the best of Tuscany's vineyards.

9 Ristorante Fiorentino, Sansepolcro

Sansepolcro's best restaurant *(see p107)* is over 200 years old – an old-fashioned, wood-ceilinged, homey trattoria of Tuscan cuisine. The owner prefers to rhapsodize about what's best in the kitchen today rather than handing customers a menu, and enjoys discussing the works of Piero della Francesca.

10 Trattoria Sant'Omobono, Pisa

Simple and traditional Pisan home cooking is offered at this hidden gem *(see p113)* of a trattoria in the outdoor market. The menu is full of long-standing Pisan favourites such as *baccalá* (salt cod), *coniglio* (rabbit) and *brachetti alla renaiola*, an ancient recipe of pasta squares in puréed turnip greens and smoked fish.

TOP 10 Tuscany for Free

Relaxing in the Cascate del Mulino

1 Saturnia Hot Springs

At the Cascate del Mulino (see p66), you can splash in cobalt-blue pools under gentle waterfalls, as warm spring waters soak your skin in sulphur and other minerals. These open-air thermal springs are open all year round.

2 State Museum First Sundays

With Italy's popular #DomenicalMuseo program, every state museum and archaeological area in Tuscany is free on the first Sunday of the month. The list includes some of the best: Florence's Uffizi (see pp12–15) and the Galleria dell'Accademia (see p81), Piero della Francesca's frescoes in Arezzo (see p103) and Chiusi's Etruscan museum (see p122).

3 Tuscan Church Masterpieces

Some of Italy's most precious artworks are on show in Tuscan churches. In Pistoia, the tiny Church of Sant'Andrea (see p59) has Giovanni Pisano's carved stone pulpit, which dates from 1301. Pienza's stunning cathedral (see p55) is one of the few in Italy that has its original gold-leaf altarpieces still in place, rather than installed in a museum.

4 Gregorian Chant

In the church of San Miniato al Monte (see p53) in Florence and the Romanesque abbey of Sant'Antimo (see p54) near Montalcino, monks still celebrate daily prayer in chant. You can find the exact schedules at the tourist offices.

5 Free Tour Florence
www.freetourflorence.com

Free guided walks around Florence depart from outside Santa Maria Novella every day. In the morning tour, Medici rulers and their palaces take centre stage while in the afternoon the focus is on Renaissance architecture and outdoor local markets. Donations are welcome and reservations are required.

6 Pilgrims' Path
www.viefrancigene.org/en

The Via Francigena was the medieval pilgrims' route from Canterbury to Rome, and much of the path through Tuscany has been waymarked for 21st-century walkers. The 30-km (19-mile) stretch between San Gimignano and Monteriggioni is among the most picturesque. The website has downloadable maps.

Pilgrims' Path

7 A Village with a View

The ancient Etruscan settlement of Fiesole is ideally situated for a panorama over Florence in the valley below. A little balcony on the steep road to San Francesco monastery is the perfect spot to snap the city and Chianti hills beyond.

8 Abbazia di Monte Oliveto Maggiore

The Great Cloister at this remote monastery (see p122) has over 30 narrative panels painted by Renaissance artists Luca Signorelli and Sodoma. The drive there, through the surreal landscape of the Crete Senesi hills, is a Tuscan classic.

9 Archivio di Stato di Siena

From the 1250s to the beginning of the 18th century, Siena's local government commissioned illustrations for the front cover of the city ledger, often from top-rank artists like Ambrogio Lorenzetti and Sano di Pietro. You can see these "Tavolette di Biccherna" on guided visits around the Archivio di Stato (see p97) or state archive.

Detail, Pontormo's *Entombment*

10 Mannerist Masterpieces

The big names of the art movement that grew around Michelangelo were all Florentines: Andrea del Sarto, Pontormo and Rosso Fiorentino. Key works are scattered around city churches and cloisters, including Santissima Annunziata (see p53), Santa Felicità and the Chiostro dello Scalzo.

TOP 10 BUDGET TIPS

Refreshing Italian gelato

1 Give heavy desserts a miss and have a much cheaper and more refreshing gelato instead.

2 At coffee bars and cafés, a *caffè al banco* (coffee had standing at the counter) costs a fraction of a *caffè al tavolo* (at the table).

3 *Aperitivo* or "happy hour" buffets are unlimited from around 7 to 9pm. Buy a drink, eat your fill from the ample buffet and skip dinner.

4 Eat lunch at markets frequented by locals, such as Florence's Sant'Ambrogio (*www.mercatosantambrogio.it*) or the Central Market (*www.mercatocentrale. it/firenze*).

5 When booking accommodation, don't be afraid to haggle with the hotel by email. Booking directly with them saves them commission fees.

6 You'll get more accommodation for your money in less attractive areas (such as around Florence's train station) or in hostels or monasteries. Look at Monastery Stays (see p141) for details.

7 If you are a visitor from outside the EU, you can get a refund on the 22 per cent sales tax (known as IVA) on goods purchased. Save your shopping for one big store to hurdle the €155 lower limit for a tax refund (see p140).

8 The low season runs from mid-October to March. Airfares and hotel prices drop, although coastal resorts are deserted.

9 Long-distance rail fares are much cheaper when booked between 90 and 120 days in advance.

10 Thursday is a popular evening for free talks at many museums, including at Florence's Strozzina. Find details at www.strozzina.org.

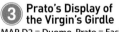 Festivals

1 Viareggio's Carnevale

MAP C2 ■ Viale Carducci and Viale Marconi, Viareggio ■ Shrove Tue, and weekends in Lent

This carnival may lack the costumed balls of Venice, but their parade of elaborate floats is almost as famous.

2 Florence's Scoppio del Carro

MAP M3 ■ Piazza di S Giovanni, Florence ■ Easter Sun

White oxen pull a firework-laden cart from the Baptistry's *Gates of Paradise* to the Duomo. During Easter mass, a mechanical dove sails on a wire down the nave and through the door to ignite the cart in an explosion of noise and colour.

Float, Viareggio Carnevale

3 Prato's Display of the Virgin's Girdle

MAP D2 ■ Duomo, Prato ■ Easter, 1 May, 15 Aug, 8 Sep, 25 Dec

When the Virgin was assumed, body and soul, to Heaven, Doubting Thomas was sceptical, so she gave him her girdle as proof of her ascent. Legend has it that the girdle was eventually inherited by a woman from Jerusalem who married a man from Prato, who brought it to the town in the 12th century. It was later encased in a glass-and-gold reliquary, and locked in the Duomo. Five times a year the bishop shows it to those in the piazza and church, and lets the faithful kiss the case. A procession is then led by musicians in Renaissance-style costumes.

4 Maggio Musicale and Estate Fiesolana

Various venues ■ May–Aug ■ www.maggiofiorentino. com, www.bitconcerti.it/ estate-fiesolana-2022.html

May and June bring concerts, plays and recitals to Florence's theatres, churches and public spaces. From June to August, Estate Fiesolana hosts performing arts events in Fiesole; best of all are those held under the stars in the ancient Roman theatre high above the town.

5 Florence's Queer Festival

MAP N1 ■ Cinema La Compagnia ■ Mid-Oct

The Florence Queer Festival has become one of the most important LGBTQ+ festivals in Italy. It is dedicated to promoting LGBTQ+ culture through cinema, video, theatre, photography and literature.

6 Florence's Calcio Storico

MAP P4 ■ Piazza Santa Croce, Florence ■ 16–29 Jun

Played between Florence's four traditional neighbourhoods, this is football without the rules. A violent game – with players dressed in

Costumed drummers at Florence's Calcio Storico festival

Renaissance costume – this is usually played on the dusty Piazza Santa Croce, with matches in past years taking place in Piazza della Signoria or the Boboli Gardens.

7 Pisa's Gioco del Ponte
MAP C3 ▪ Ponte di Mezzo ▪ Last weekend in Jun

Pisan residents from either side of the Arno have always been rivals. During this festival they act out this rivalry and fight it out by dressing in Renaissance costumes and staging an inverse tug-of-war on Pisa's oldest bridge, trying to push a giant, leaden cart over to the other team's side.

8 Siena's Palio
MAP E4 ▪ Piazza del Campo, Siena ▪ 2 Jul, 16 Aug

The Palio is Siena's famous bi-annual equestrian event – which animal rights activists have long advocated to end. It's been around since the Middle Ages and involves a bareback horse race around the Campo. The festivities last for a week. On the day of the race, you can stand in the centre of the Campo for free or buy a seat ticket (months in advance) from any business ringing the piazza. Enjoy the pageantry and *sbandieratori* (flag tossers), before glimpsing the furious, 90-second race.

9 Montepulciano's Bravio delle Botti
MAP F4 ▪ Main drag ▪ Last Sun in Aug

After a week of medieval pageantry, festivities and feasting, costumed two-person teams from the town's eight neighbourhoods prove their racing prowess by rolling hefty barrels up this hill town's mean-dering, often steep main street to the piazza at the top.

Bravio delle Botti, Montepulciano

10 Montalcino's Sagra del Tordo
MAP E4 ▪ Fortezza ▪ Last weekend Oct

Part of this celebration of ancient hunting traditions is a food festival in the medieval *fortezza*, with roasted thrushes, polenta and Brunello wine.

Florence and Tuscany Area by Area

Inside the Cortile del Michelozzo in
Palazzo Vecchio, Florence

🔟 Florence

Florence is the cradle of the Renaissance, the city of Michelangelo's *David* and Botticelli's *Birth of Venus*. It was here that the Italian language was formalized and its literature born under Dante. Here, enlightened Medici princes ruled and nurtured the arts: Lorenzo the Magnificent encouraged Michelangelo to pick up a hammer and chisel, and Cosimo II protected Galileo from the Inquisition. Today, its historic core is a UNESCO World Heritage Site. Other sensory delights include Dante's medieval neighbourhood, the Oltrarno artisan quarter, the sprawling Boboli Gardens and the hilltop Fiesole.

Statue, Pitti Palace

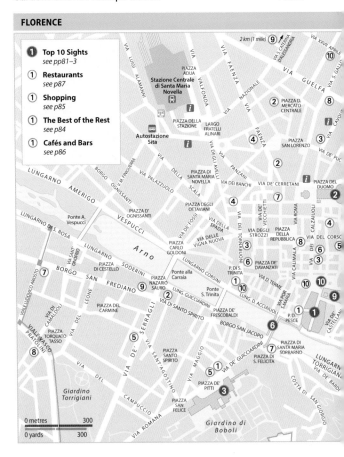

FLORENCE

1 **Top 10 Sights**
see pp81–3

1 **Restaurants**
see p87

1 **Shopping**
see p85

1 **The Best of the Rest**
see p84

1 **Cafés and Bars**
see p86

0 metres 300
0 yards 300

1 Uffizi
The greatest gallery *(see pp12–15)* of Renaissance art on earth, a veritable living textbook of Western art's most shining moments, showcasing masterpieces from Giotto and Botticelli through Michelangelo, Raphael and Leonardo da Vinci to Titian, Caravaggio and Gentileschi.

2 The Duomo Group
Visit Florence's religious heart: Giotto's lithe bell tower, the Baptistry's glimmering *Gates of Paradise* and vibrant Byzantine mosaics, as well as the Duomo

The beautiful Duomo buildings

museum's splendid Michelangelo and Donatello sculptures – all lorded over by Brunelleschi's dome *(see pp16–17)*, a miracle of Renaissance engineering and architecture.

3 Pitti Palace
This brawny Mannerist mansion *(see pp18–21)* served as Florence's royal home from 1560 until the 1860s, when Florence did a stint as Italy's capital. Backed by the beautiful and elaborate Boboli Gardens, the seven museums in the palace include the excellent Galleria Palatina of late Renaissance/early Baroque paintings.

4 Galleria dell'Accademia
MAP N1 ■ Via Ricasoli 60 ■ Open 9am–6pm Tue–Sun ■ Adm ■ www.galleriaaccademia firenze.beniculturali.it

Michelangelo's *David* stands pensively at the end of a corridor lined by the artist's *Slaves (see p56)*.

***David* at the Galleria dell'Accademia**

THE BONFIRE OF THE VANITIES

The puritanical preacher Girolamo Savonarola took advantage of a weak Medici to seize power in 1494. The iron-fisted "Mad Monk's" reign peaked in 1497 when his bands of boys looted wealthy houses to create a giant "Bonfire of the Vanities" on Piazza della Signoria. A year later, under threat of excommunication, Florence burned Savonarola himself at the stake at the same spot as the monk's bonfire.

5 Santa Croce

MAP P4–P5 ▪ Piazza S Croce ▪ Open 9:30am–5:30pm Mon–Sat, 12:30–5:45pm Sun & hols ▪ Adm includes museum

The tombs of Galileo and Michelangelo, as well as Giotto frescoes and a renowned leatherworking school (see p85) can be found here (see p52). Located close to the lovely cloisters are a Renaissance chapel designed by Brunelleschi (decorated by Luca della Robbia), and a small museum with a *Last Supper* by Taddeo Gaddi and a *Crucifix* by Cimabue, restored after the flood of 1966.

***Il Pescatore* at Il Bargello**

6 Ponte Vecchio

MAP M4–M5 ▪ Via Por S Maria/ Via Guicciardini

The shops hanging from both sides of Taddeo Gaddi's 1345 "old bridge" have housed gold- and silversmiths since Ferdinando I evicted the butchers in the 16th century (his private corridor passed overhead, and he couldn't stand the smell). Even the Nazis, blowing up bridges to slow the Allied advance, found the span too beautiful to destroy and instead took down the buildings at either end.

7 San Marco

MAP N1 ▪ Piazza di S Marco 1 ▪ Open 8:15am–1:50pm Mon–Sat, 1st & 3rd Mon and 2nd, 4th & 5th Sun of month ▪ Adm

Cosimo il Vecchio de' Medici commissioned Michelozzo to build this Dominican monastery in 1437. Fra Angelico lived here and frescoed the cells of his fellow monks with devotional images and left a plethora of golden altarpieces that are now housed inside the Renaissance monastery's old Pilgrim's Hospice. A portrait of Savonarola by Fra Bartolomeo hangs in the "Mad Monk's" room, next to a scene of the theocrat's fiery death.

8 Il Bargello

MAP N4 ▪ Via del Proconsolo 4 ▪ Open 8:15am–1:50pm Mon & Wed–Fri, 1st, 3rd & 5th Sun of the month ▪ Adm

Florence's sculpture gallery, installed in a medieval former town hall and prison, contains some early works of Michelangelo, Mannerist Giambologna's gravity-defying *Flying Mercury* (1564) and an engaging Donatello collection, including *David* in marble and *David* in bronze (the first nude since antiquity) and a *St George* (1416).

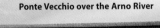

Ponte Vecchio over the Arno River

Palazzo Vecchio's stone façade

9 Palazzo Vecchio

MAP N4 ■ Piazza della
Signoria 1 ■ Museum & tower: open
9am–7pm Fri–Wed (until 2pm Thu);
book a ticket ahead of visit at www.
bigliettimusei.comune.fi.it ■ Adm

Arnolfo di Cambio's mighty town hall
(1299–1302) is still the seat of
government. Vasari, who was
hired by Cosimo I to redecorate
the medieval palace in the 1540s,
frescoed a Medici marriage around
Michelozzo's 1453 courtyard and
swathed the Sala dei Cinquecento
with an apotheosis of the Medici
dynasty. Francesco I shut himself
away from matters of state in his
barrel-vaulted Studiolo to conduct
scientific experiments. Note that
children under 6 are not permitted.

10 Piazza della Signoria

MAP N4

Florence's living room and sculpture
gallery is home to the *Neptune* fountain
by Ammannati, which was dismissed
by Michelangelo as a "waste of good
marble". On the *arringheria* – the platform from which orators "harangued"
the crowds – are copies of Donatello's
Marzocco (Florence's leonine symbol)
and *Judith*, and Michelangelo's *David*.
The only original, Bandinelli's 1534
Hercules, was derided by Cellini as a
"sack of melons". Orcagna's 14th-cen-
tury Loggia dei Lanzi shelters Cellini's
Perseus (1545) and Giambologna's
Rape of the Sabine Women (1583).

THE BEST OF FLORENCE

▶ MORNING

Book your **Accademia** *(055 294
883)* tickets *(see p81)* for 9am
and spend some time perusing
the many paintings and
Michelangelo statues. Next make
your way towards the **Duomo**
(see pp16–17). Aim to be at the
Museo dell'Opera del Duomo
(see p17) around 11am, then head
to the Duomo itself and climb
the dome for stupendous views.
Wander past the **Baptistry** *(see
p16)* to gaze upon its dazzling
bronze doors. Stroll down the Via
dei Calzaiuoli and turn left onto
Via dei Cimatori for lunch from
I Fratellini *(see p86)*, nibbling your
sandwich and sipping wine while
lounging on the cobbled street.

AFTERNOON

During *pausa pranzo* (lunch break),
trek over to the basilica of **Santa
Croce** to pay your respects to the
artistic luminaries buried there,
and to browse the leather shop.
On your way back to the heart
of town, stop at the **Gelateria
dei Neri** *(Via dei Neri 9/11r)*, one
of Florence's best gelato parlours,
for a fortifying triple scoop. Have
Uffizi *(see pp12–15)* reservations
for 4pm: this will give you enough
time to explore before closing
time. Afterwards, take a stroll
across the charming **Ponte
Vecchio** in the twilight, pause
to gaze at the Arno River, then
plunge into the **Oltrarno** district
to find a good spot for dinner – try
Pizzeria Berberè in the Piazza de'
Nerli 1 for Italian craft beers and
some of the best pizzas in town.

See map on pp80–81

The Best of the Rest

1 Churches
Florence's major churches are covered fully on pp52–3, and the Duomo on pp16–17.

2 Museo Archeologico
MAP P2 ■ Piazza Santissima Annunziata 9B ■ Open 8:30am–2pm Mon–Wed & Sat, 1:30–7pm Thu & Fri ■ Adm

Fascinating Etruscan artifacts on display here (see p44) include a silver amphora from Antioch, a wooden Hittite chariot and the Roman bronze *Idolino*.

Lion's head, Museo Archeologico

3 Palazzo Medici-Riccardi
MAP N2 ■ Via Cavour 1 ■ Open 9am–7pm Thu–Tue ■ Adm

A must-see in this Medici palace of 1444 are the chapel's 360° frescoes by Benozzo Gozzoli.

4 Casa Buonarroti
MAP P4 ■ Via Ghibellina 70 ■ Open 10am–4:30pm Wed–Mon ■ Adm

Carvings by Michelangelo are on display at his nephew's house, along with works by Baroque artists including Artemisia Gentileschi.

5 Casa di Dante
MAP N3 ■ Via S Margherita 1 ■ Open Apr–Oct: 10am–6pm daily; Nov–Mar: 10am–5pm Tue–Fri ■ Adm

Dante is said to have been born in a house that stood here. The current building serves as a museum with displays about Dante and medieval Florence. His beloved Beatrice is buried in the church across the street.

6 Museo Horne
MAP N5 ■ Via dei Benci 6 ■ Opening hours vary, check website ■ Adm ■ www.museohorne.it

This private collection includes works by Giotto and Beccafumi.

7 Piazzale Michelangelo
MAP Q6 ■ Piazzale Michelangelo

Take in the sweeping, postcard-ready panoramas of Florence from this popular viewpoint.

8 Spedale degli Innocenti
MAP P2 ■ Piazza SS Annunziata 12 ■ Open 11am–6pm Wed–Mon ■ Adm

Europe's first orphanage, this building was designed by Brunelleschi. Its portico features terracotta foundlings by Andrea della Robbia. The museum inside houses paintings by Piero di Cosimo, Botticelli and Ghirlandaio.

9 Museo Stibbert
Wacky museum renowned for its armour collections (see p69).

10 Cenacolo di Sant'Apollonia
MAP N1 ■ Via XXVII Aprile 1 ■ Open 8:15am–1:50pm Mon–Fri; closed 1 Jan, 25 Dec, 1st, 3rd, 5th Sat & Sun of month

This former Benedictine convent holds Andrea del Castagno's dramatic 1450 *Last Supper*. Note the turbulent marble panel behind the heads of Jesus and Judas.

Andrea del Castagno's *Last Supper*

Shopping

Ferragamo store and museum

1 Ferragamo
MAP M3 ▪ Piazza Santa
Trinita 5r; open 10:30am–7:30pm
daily ▪ Adm ▪ www.ferragamo.com

This flagship store and museum for
luxury shoes dates back to the golden
era of the 1920s.

2 San Lorenzo Market
MAP M2 ▪ Piazza del Mercato
Centrale ▪ Open 9am–midnight daily
▪ www.mercatocentrale.com

This outdoor market offers
a range of leather and
paper goods as well
as fashion items. The
adjacent food market
is open every morning
except Sunday.

3 Gucci
MAP M3 ▪ Via
dei Tornabuoni 73r–81r
▪ Open 10am–7:30pm Mon–Sat
(until 7pm Sun) ▪ www.gucci.com

Guccio Gucci's main Firenze store
initially sold leather accessories – it
now sells a range of the brand's
contemporary collections.

La Botteghina platter

4 Enoteca Alessi
MAP N3 ▪ Via delle Oche 27r
▪ Open 10:30am–7pm daily ▪ www.
enotecaalessi.it

This sweet shop's basement wine
merchant is the best in town.

5 Pitti Mosaici
MAP L5 ▪ Piazza de' Pitti 23r
▪ 055 282 127 (call ahead for reservations) ▪ www.pittimosaici.com

Quality *pietre dure* – "mosaics" of
semiprecious stones – are sold here.

6 Emilio Pucci
MAP M3 ▪ Via Tornabuoni 20r
▪ Open 10am–7pm daily ▪ www.
emiliopucci.com

Emilio Pucci's fashion house has
offered daring prints for decades.

7 Casa dei Tessuti
MAP M3 ▪ Via de' Pecori 20–24r
▪ Open 10am–1pm & 3–7pm Mon–
Sat ▪ www.casadeitessuti.com

Wonderful selection of textiles,
with a few designer names.
Occasional talks on Florence
are held in the shop.

8 La Botteghina del Ceramista
MAP M1 ▪ Via Guelfa 5r ▪ Opening
hours vary, check website ▪ www.
labotteghinadelceramista.it

Hand-painted ceramics
from some of central
Italy's best artisans.

9 Scuola del Cuoio di Santa Croce
MAP P4 ▪ Piazza di
Santa Croce (inside
church); on Sun enter at
Via di San Giuseppe 5r
▪ Open 10am–6:30pm
daily ▪ www.leatherschool.biz

High-quality, butter-soft leather
products by local artisans. All
purchases are monogrammed
in gold leaf.

10 Pineider
MAP M4 ▪ Lungarno degli
Acciaiuoli 72r ▪ Open 10am–7pm
daily ▪ www.pineider.com

Founded in 1774, Pineider sells
elegant hand-engraved stationery
and personalized leather goods.

See map on pp80–81

Cafés and Bars

The Pitti Gola e Cantina wine bar

1 Pitti Gola e Cantina
MAP L5 ■ Piazza Pitti 16
■ www.pittigolaecantina.com
A refined wine bar with good snacks situated right by the splendid Pitti Palace and its treasure-trove of art.

2 Il Santino
MAP L4 ■ Via Santo Spirito 60
■ www.ilsantobevitore.com
On one of the Left Bank's hippest streets, this wine bar serves tasty Florentine tapas to complement a short, but expertly chosen, wine list.

3 I Fratellini
MAP N4 ■ Via dei Cimatori 38r
■ 055 239 6096
This *fiaschetteria* – a hole-in-the-wall wine bar – also serves some delicious sandwiches for on-the-go street-side eating while you're out and about.

4 BrewDog
MAP P5 ■ Via Faenza 21/r
■ 055 217 035
Scottish BrewDog is at the centre of Florence's craft beer scene, headlining a unique range of international speciality and guest brews.

5 Archea
MAP K5 ■ Via de' Serragli 44r
■ www.archeapub.com
A small Belgian-style pub, Archea has its own microbrewery and offers good European craft beers.

6 Cantinetta dei Verrazzano
MAP N3–N4 ■ Via dei Tavolini 18r
■ www.verrazzano.com/la-cantinetta-in-firenze
Try great pastries and stuffed *focaccia* sandwiches at this café-bar owned by the Chianti wine estate (see p40).

7 Le Volpi e l'Uva
MAP M5 ■ Piazza dei Rossi 1
■ www.levolpieluva.com
A low-key, jazzy wine bar in the Oltrarno antiques and artisan district.

8 La Terrazza
MAP M3 ■ Inside Hotel Continentale, Lungarno degli Acciaiuoli, 2r ■ 055 283 612
Take in the view over the rooftops of Florence and the hills beyond from this tiny terrace café.

9 La Cité Libreria Café
MAP K4 ■ Borgo San Frediano 20r ■ 3499 011 105
This bohemian café-bookshop turns into a relaxed bar by night. It also serves as an eclectic events space.

10 Rivoire
MAP N4 ■ Piazza della Signoria 5r ■ www.rivoire.it
Soak up Italy in style at this classy chocolatier's café with tables right on the Piazza della Signoria.

Rivoire on the Piazza della Signoria

Restaurants

The stylish interior of Ora d'Aria

PRICE CATEGORIES

For a three-course meal for one with half
a bottle of wine (or equivalent meal),
taxes and extra charges.

€ under €35   €€ €35–70   €€€ over €70

① Ora d'Aria
MAP M4 ■ Via dei Georgofili 11r ■ 055 200 1699 ■ Closed Sun ■ €€€

Head chef Marco Stabile cooks up creative Tuscan haute cuisine at this Michelin-starred establishment.

② Konnubio
MAP M2 ■ Via dei Conti 8r ■ 055 238 1189 ■ €€

Elegant but affable dining is offered here (see p72) with Tuscan and vegan dishes on the menu.

③ Zeb
MAP P6 ■ Via San Miniato 2r ■ 055 234 2864 ■ Closed Wed & Sun D ■ €€

This restaurant offers traditional Tuscan dishes made with the freshest ingredients. The filled pastas are sublime.

④ Cantinetta Antinori
MAP L3 ■ Piazza Antinori 3 ■ 055 292 234 ■ Closed Sun ■ €€€

A wine bar and restaurant (see p70) set within a 15th-century palazzo. The Antinori family has been making Chianti for generations, and the produce comes from their farms.

⑤ Sud
Via Villamagna, 41/a ■ 0556 530 281 ■ €

Situated inside Anconella park, Sud serves excellent wood-fired pizza, along with a daily seasonal menu.

⑥ Antica Trattoria da Tito
Via San Gallo 112r ■ 055 472 475 ■ €€

Theatrical and genuine, this popular neighbourhood trattoria offers a traditional taste of old Florence.

⑦ iO: Osteria Personale
MAP J4 ■ Borgo San Frediano 167r ■ 055 933 1341 ■ Closed Sun ■ €€€

Expect contemporary dishes that are created using classic Tuscan produce such as octopus or *Cinta Senese* pork.

Sorbet at iO: Osteria Personale

⑧ Alla Vecchia Bettola
MAP J5 ■ Viale Vasco Pratolini 3/5/7 ■ 055 224 158 ■ Closed Sun & Mon ■ €€

Old-fashioned dishes, such as *testicciole* (stew in a halved sheep skull), are served here.

⑨ Il Pizzaiuolo
MAP Q4 ■ Via dei Macci 113r ■ 055 241 171 ■ Closed Sun ■ €

This crowded pizza parlour also served tasty Neapolitan pasta dishes. Expect a wait even with reservations.

⑩ Brac
MAP N5 ■ Via dei Vagellai 18r ■ 055 094 4877 ■ €

A delightful vegetarian and vegan restaurant with a romantic courtyard.

See map on pp80–81

🔟 Around Florence

The lush hills and wide Arno Valley spreading out from Florence are overlooked by most travellers making a beeline for Siena and Pisa. Skip the main roads and discover the spots known only to locals. There's no lovelier route to Siena than the S222 Chiantigiana through the famed terracotta centre Impruneta to the castle-topped, vine-clad hills of the Chianti wine region. Just off the road to Pisa, the towns of Prato and Pistoia would be better known for their rich heritages of Romanesque architecture and Renaissance art were they not overshadowed by their mighty neighbours. Villas built by the Medici dot the countryside northwest of town.

Sculpture, Roman theatre, Fiesole

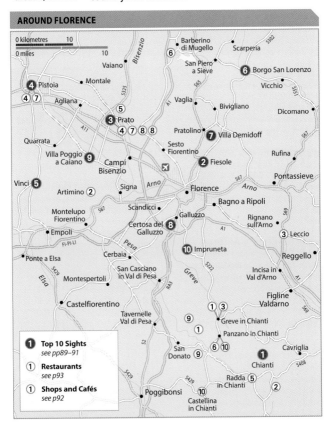

AROUND FLORENCE

0 kilometres 10
0 miles 10

Barberino di Mugello · Scarperia · S503
⑥ · San Piero a Sieve · ⑥ Borgo San Lorenzo
Vaiano · Bisenzio · Vicchio
④ ⑦ Pistoia · Montale · Vaglia · A1 · Bivigliano · Dicomano
Agliana · ⑤ · ③ Prato · ④ ⑦ ⑧ ⑧ · Pratolino · ⑦ Villa Demidoff · S67
Quarrata · Sesto Fiorentino · Rufina
Villa Poggio a Caiano ⑨ · Campi Bisenzio · ② Fiesole · Pontassieve
Vinci ⑤ · Artimino ② · Signa · Arno · Florence · Arno
Montelupo Fiorentino · Scandicci · Bagno a Ripoli · S69
Empoli · Certosa del Galluzzo ⑧ · Galluzzo · Rignano sull'Arno
Ponte a Elsa · Pesa · ⑩ Impruneta · ③ Leccio
Cerbaia · Reggello
Montespertoli · San Casciano in Val di Pesa · Greve · Incisa in Val d'Arno
Castelfiorentino · Tavernelle Val di Pesa · Figline Valdarno
⑨ · ① ③ · S69
San Donato ⑨ · ⑥ ⑩ · Greve in Chianti · Cavriglia
① · Panzano in Chianti · S408
Chianti · ①
Poggibonsi · ⑩ · Radda in Chianti ⑤ · ②
Castellina in Chianti

① Top 10 Sights
see pp89–91

① Restaurants
see p93

① Shops and Cafés
see p92

Vineyards stretching to the horizon in the Chianti region of Tuscany

1 Chianti

Tuscany's famous wine region *(see pp38–41)* has vineyards and castles, market towns and monasteries.

2 Fiesole

MAP E2 ■ Tourist office: Via Portigiani Zenobi 3 ■ 0555 961 311

This hilltop Etruscan settlement *(see p61)* is a short ride from Florence on a No. 7 bus. The 11th-century cathedral was assembled using ancient Roman columns, and houses Renaissance sculptures by Giovanni della Robbia and Mino da Fiesole. The remains of a Roman theatre and baths are still used for Estate Fiesolana summer concerts. The steep road up to San Francesco church, with its quiet cloisters and quirky missionary museum, passes a popular park, shaded by ilex and filled with watercolourists reproducing its famous view of Florence.

3 Prato

MAP D2 ■ Tourist office: Piazza del Comune; 0574 183 7859; www.pratoturismo.it ■ Duomo: Piazza del Duomo; open daily ■ Museum: open Mon, Wed–Sun & hols; adm for frescoes and museum combined

The mercantile tradition of this city dates to 15th-century financial genius Francesco Datini, famed "Merchant of Prato" and inventor of the promissory note. His frescoed palazzo is one of the best preserved of its kind in Italy. Prato's finest art is in the Duomo *(see p55)*, but the Galleria Comunale has a lovely collection of early Renaissance polyptych altarpieces by such masters as Filippo Lippi and Bernardo Daddi. The Castello dell'Imperatore (1420s), its ramparts and grassy interior now a city park, was built by Emperor Frederick II to defend the road from his German kingdom to his lands in southern Italy.

4 Pistoia

MAP D2 ■ Tourist office: Piazza Duomo 1; 057 321 622; www.turismo.pistoia.eu ■ Duomo: Piazza Duomo; open daily; adm for St Jacopo's chapel

Pistoia, an ancient Roman town of metalworkers, is known for its thin daggers, which became handguns. These were called *pistole* after the city. It is an artistic crossroads where the Romanesque stripes in San Giovanni Fuoricivitas and the Duomo *(see p55)* meet the Florentine Renaissance glazed terracottas festooning the Ospedale del Ceppo. Gothic art comes in the form of colourful 1372 frescoes covering the Cappella del Tau, and a Giovanni Pisano carved pulpit (1298–1301) in the church of Sant'Andrea.

Aerial view of the Duomo, Pistoia

Appennino's statue in Pratolino park at Villa Demidoff

5 Vinci
MAP D2 ▪ Tourist office:
Via Montalbano 1; 0571 933 285

One of the greatest scientific minds and artistic talents in history, Leonardo da Vinci, was born on the outskirts of this medieval hill town in 1452. The 11th-century Castello Guidi houses a Museo Vinciano with over 100 models of the master's inventions. Up the road, set in a picturesque olive-clad farmscape is his *casa natale* (birthplace) that seems straight from one of Leonardo's works.

6 Borgo San Lorenzo
Tourist office: MAP E2; Piazzale Lavacchini; 0558 456 230 ▪ Villa: MAP D3; Via Ponti Medicei 7, Cerreto Guidi; 057 155 707; open daily, call ahead for opening hours

Surrounded by Medici villas such as Villa Medicea di Cerreto Guidi *(see p65)* and the Michelozzo-designed Castello del Trebbio (1461), this town was rebuilt after a 1919 earthquake. The 12th-century Pieve di San Lorenzo church contains Renaissance altarpieces by Taddeo Gaddi and Bachiacca, a damaged *Madonna* fresco by Giotto and apse murals by local Art Nouveau ceramics entrepreneur Galileo Chini (1906).

Statue, Pieve di San Lorenzo

7 Villa Demidoff
MAP E2 ▪ Pratolino ▪ 055 409 427 ▪ Open Apr–Nov: 10am–8pm Fri– Sun & hols (Oct: until 6pm) ▪ Adm

The original Villa di Pratolino *(see p65)* is gone, but Bernardo Buontalenti's fountain-filled Pratolino park remains a favourite excursion from Florence.

8 Certosa del Galluzzo
MAP E3 ▪ Galluzzo ▪ Guided tours only: 10am, 11am, 1pm, 4pm & 7pm Tue–Sat (Nov: 3pm & 4pm only), 3pm & 4pm Sun

Established in 1341, this charterhouse was home to Carthusian monks until 1956. It serves monks of the Cistercian Order now. The building retains an original small monk's church, a visitable cell and Renaissance cloisters set with della Robbia terracotta *tondi* and a gallery of the Pontormo frescoes dating from 1523–5.

9 Villa Poggio a Caiano
MAP D2 ▪ Piazza de' Medici 14, Poggio a Caiano ▪ 055 877 012 ▪ Open 8:30am– 3:30pm Tue–Wed, Fri–Sat, 2nd & 3rd Sun of month

This ultimate Renaissance Medici villa *(see p64)* was designed by Giuliano da Sangallo at the end of the 15th century for Lorenzo the Magnificent.

FLORENTINE EXPANSION

In 1125, Florence virtually obliterated its hilltop neighbour Fiesole and began to prowl for land. It allied with the amenable (Prato, 1351), conquered the recalcitrant (Pistoia, 1301; Pisa, 1406) and built the rest (Livorno, 1571). After three years of bloody battle Siena was finally defeated (1554–7), and in 1569, the Medici pope Pius V named Cosimo I de' Medici the Grand Duke of Tuscany.

Also known as Ambra, the villa is a UNESCO World Heritage Site. It houses two museums inside its halls.

⑩ Impruneta
MAP E3 ■ Tourist office: Via Cavalleggeri 29 ■ 0552 313 729

This terracotta-producing town is famed for its Renaissance collegiate church of Santa Maria. Flanking the high altar are chapels designed by Michelozzo and decorated with Luca della Robbia terracottas. The one on the right contains a fragment of the True Cross, the left an icon of the Virgin (supposedly painted by St Luke), buried here during the early Christian persecutions and dug up when the church foundations were laid. Also on view are fine Baroque paintings and a Mannerist crucifix by Giambologna.

Santa Maria church, Impruneta

A TOUR OF THE REGION

▶ **MORNING**

Start with **Pistoia** *(see p89)* and the stupendous Gothic frescoes inside Capella del Tau (incredibly, a private owner in the 16th century whilewashed over them). Go down to zebra-striped San Giovanni Fuoricivitas for a Romanesque feast.

It's a short walk to see Pistoia's octagonal Baptistry, designed (maybe) by Andrea Pisano and unmistakable with its hoops of green and white marble. Don't dawdle: you need time for the Duomo opposite *(see p89)* then Sant'Andrea (closes 12:30). Head back to the centre by way of the Ospedale del Ceppo and its colourful glazed terracotta frieze. Eat lunch at long-standing local favourite La BotteGaia *(see p93)* just off the picturesque market square where medieval-style second storeys project over the ground floors of the buildings.

AFTERNOON

From Pistoia, it's a quick drive to **Prato** *(see p89)*. Stop first at Palazzo Datini's frescoes (the St Christopher by the door was a common feature, believed to help protect those leaving the house) to pay your respects to the medieval "Merchant of Prato", who inscribed his account ledgers "For God and Profit".

Visit the Duomo *(see p89)* and, if you have the time, the adjacent Museo dell'Opera del Duomo and the Palazzo Pretorio. Grab a bag of *cantucci* (biscuits) at Antonio Mattei and clamber onto the broken ramparts of Castello dell'Imperatore for views of Santa Maria delle Carceri (1485–1506), a fine High Renaissance church.

See map on p88 ←

Shops and Cafés

Shoppers at Antica Macelleria Falorni

① Antica Macelleria Falorni, Greve
MAP E3 ■ Piazza Matteotti 66–67
■ www.falorni.it

The walls at this butcher's *(see p38)* have displayed prosciutto and salami since 1729. They have good wines too.

② Ceramiche Rampini, near Radda
MAP E3 ■ Casa Beretone di Vistarenni (road to Siena) ■ www.rampini ceramics.com

One of the best Italian ceramicists, producing whimsical designs.

③ The Mall, Leccio Reggello, near Florence
MAP E3 ■ Via Europa 8 (Incisa-Reggello exit from A1) ■ Open 10am–7pm daily ■ www.firenze.themall.it

Find big savings on designer wear. The building is well signposted and is 3 miles (5 km) off the main road.

④ Antonio Mattei, Prato
MAP D2 ■ Via Ricasoli 20–22
■ www.antoniomattei.com

Since 1858, this shop has been making the best *cantucci* (biscuits) in Italy. Do buy some to take back home.

⑤ Luciano Porciatti, Radda
MAP E3 ■ Piazza IV Novembre 1
■ www.casaporciatti.it/

An excellent deli featuring fine cheeses and meats.

⑥ Barberino Designer Outlet, Barberino di Mugello
MAP E2 ■ Via Meucci ■ www.mc arthurglen.com

There are over 100 high-end designer outlets, and several cafés and restaurants here.

⑦ Nuovo Mondo, Prato
MAP D2 ■ Via Garibaldi 23
■ Closed Mon D & Sun D ■ www. pasticcerianuovomondo.com

Stop by for delicious sweets, panini and pastries with classy service if you find yourself in this shopping street.

⑧ Luca Mannori, Prato
MAP D2 ■ Via Lazzerini 2
■ Closed Tue D & Sun L ■ www. pasticceriamannoriprato.it

Delicious cakes and a huge variety of chocolates are sold at this pastry shop and chocolate-makers.

Sweet treats at Luca Mannori

⑨ Cappelletti Pelletteria, Castellina in Chianti
MAP E3 ■ Via Ferruccio 43
■ www.chiantileather1893.com

Run by the same family since 1893, this traditional *pelletteria* has handmade shoes, bags and other leather goods.

⑩ Enoteca Baldi, Panzano
MAP E3 ■ Piazza Bucciarelli 25
■ www.enotecabaldi.it

Located on the town's main square, this lively wine bar is the perfect place to enjoy a glass of local wine with a plate of bruschetta.

Restaurants

1 **La Cantinetta di Rignana, near Greve**
MAP E3 ■ Loc Rignana ■ 3474 534 884 ■ €€

Deep in the countryside, set (see p73) among vineyards, this is the ultimate in rural feasting: both the setting and the food are second to none.

2 **Da Delfina, Artimino**
MAP D2 ■ Via della Chiesa 1 ■ 055 871 8074 ■ Closed Mon ■ €€

This is one of Tuscany's finest countryside restaurants, mixing classy service with refined but traditional cooking. *Coniglio con olive e pinoli*, rabbit with olives and pine nuts, is a speciality.

3 **Enoteca Ristorante Gallo Nero, Greve in Chianti**
MAP E3 ■ Via Battisti 9 ■ 055 853 734 ■ Closed Thu ■ €€

A wide selection of meat dishes, homemade pastas and a good wine list are offered at this friendly, family-run restaurant.

4 **La BotteGaia, Pistoia**
MAP D2 ■ Via del Lastrone 17 ■ 0573 365 602 ■ Closed Mon ■ €€

This long-standing local favourite is a traditional Slow Food *osteria* serving the cuisine of northern Tuscany.

5 **La Fontana, Prato**
MAP D2 ■ Via del Canneto 1 ■ 0574 27 282 ■ €€

La Fontana specializes in simple Tuscan food with a variety of fragrant home-baked desserts. Portions are generous and prices reasonable.

6 **Oltre il Giardino, Panzano**
MAP E3 ■ Piazza G Bucciarelli 42 ■ 055 852 828 ■ €€

Enjoy generous portions, intimacy and picture-postcard views. The menu changes daily. Advance booking is advised.

PRICE CATEGORIES

For a three-course meal for one with half a bottle of wine (or equivalent meal), taxes and extra charges.

€ under €35 €€ €35–70 €€€ over €70

7 **Osteria Via dell'Abbondanza 14, Pistoia**
MAP D2 ■ Via dell'Abbondanza 14 ■ 0573 564 655 ■ Closed Mon & Tue ■ €€

Cosy restaurant serving superb Tuscan fare. Try the glazed figs.

8 **Baghino, Prato**
MAP D2 ■ Via dell'Accademia 9 ■ 0574 27 920 ■ Closed Sun & Mon L ■ €€€

Tuscan and Italian dishes at the best restaurant in the historic town centre.

9 **L'Antica Scuderia**
MAP E3 ■ Via di Passignano 17, Badia a Passignano ■ 055 807 1623 ■ Closed Tue ■ €€

Classic Tuscan dining (see p72) amid an ocean of Chianti vines.

10 **Albergaccio, Castellina**
MAP E3 ■ Via Fiorentina 63 ■ 0577 741 042 ■ Closed Sun ■ €€€

A creative, nouvelle touch is given to Tuscan dishes, such as ricotta gnocchi under shaved black truffles and thyme.

Elegant interiors of Albergaccio

See map on p88 ←

TOP 10 Siena

Siena offers the sunny disposition of a Gothic brick-built hill town to contrast with historic rival Florence's stately Renaissance marble. Founded by the Etruscans, Siena developed during the Middle Ages in part due to the Via Francigena pilgrim route that passed through the town. As a thriving medieval merchant and textile town, Siena produced a colourful, courtly Gothic school of painting as well as a building boom, but it all came to a crashing halt when the Black Death of 1348 decimated the population. Florence dominated thereafter, but luckily for today's visitors this means that, aside from a few Baroque churches, Siena lacked the funds to overhaul its look – its exquisite medieval core is now a UNESCO World Heritage Site.

Siena's Duomo

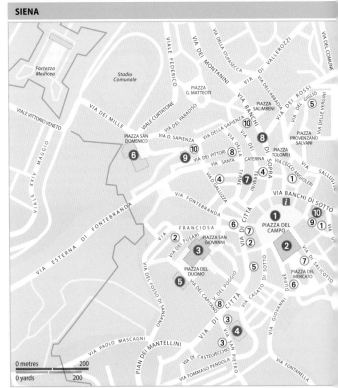

Siena's beautiful Piazza del Campo

1 Piazza del Campo

Siena's half-moon of a public square is one of the loveliest *piazze* in all of Italy, so rich in sightseeing opportunities that it counts as one of the area's unmissable sights *(see pp34–5)*. Its broad slope is home to the biannual Palio horse race *(see p77)* as well as daily streams of strollers, readers, picnickers and coffee-drinkers.

2 Palazzo Pubblico
MAP E4 ▪ Piazza del Campo ▪ Open 10am–7pm daily ▪ Adm

Siena's medieval town hall is a brick palace. The rooms were decorated with art from the early 14th-century – including Simone Martini's *Maestà* and Ambrogio Lorenzetti's *Allegory of Good and Bad Government*. They were turned into the Museo Civico *(see p36)*.

3 Duomo
MAP E4 ▪ Piazza del Duomo ▪ Open daily ▪ Adm

This massive Gothic cathedral complex, another unmissable sight *(see pp30–32)*, is filled with art by Michelangelo, Pisano, Pinturicchio, Bernini, Duccio and Donatello.

4 Pinacoteca Nazionale
MAP E4 ▪ Via S Pietro 29 ▪ Open 9am–7pm Tue–Fri ▪ Adm

The Pinacoteca *(see p57)* features an extensive collection of Sienese paintings. Seek out the 14th-century Madonnas by Simone Martini and Pietro Lorenzetti and admire Ambrogio Lorenzetti's *Annunciation*. Compare Beccafumi's cartoons (full-sized preparatory sketches on *cartone*, or "large paper") with the Duomo's floor panels and his Mannerist *Christ Descending into Limbo* to his rival Sodoma's High Renaissance works.

Detail of Lorenzetti's *Annunciation*

ST CATHERINE OF SIENA

Italy's patron saint Caterina Benincasa (1347–80) put on a nun's veil (she never took vows) after her first vision of Christ at 8; she received the stigmata at 28. Her wisdom won her the ambassadorship of Florence to Pope Gregory XI in Avignon in 1376, where she worked to convince the pope to bring back the papacy to Rome. In 1970, she became the first female Doctor of the Church.

5 Santa Maria della Scala
MAP E4 ■ Piazza del Duomo
■ Open 10am–7pm daily ■ Adm
■ www.santamariadellascala.com

This former hospital (see p32), which operated from the 9th century to the 1990s, is being transformed into one of Europe's largest cultural centres. Visitors can tour the oratories, chapels, church and museums. Several spaces host changing exhibitions. Don't miss the Renaissance frescoes in the Sala del Pellegrino, which depict scenes of hospital life not too different from today – a monkish surgeon doctoring an injured leg, another taking a urine sample, a third dozing as his patient describes symptoms.

6 San Domenico
MAP E4 ■ Piazza S Domenico
■ Open Nov–Feb: 8:30am–6pm daily (summer: from 7am daily)

This massive brick church of 1226 contains a portrait of St Catherine by her contemporary and friend Andrea Vanni. The saint's mummified head and thumb are revered in a chapel decorated with frescoes on her life by Sodoma (1526) and Francesco Vanni. Matteo di Giovanni executed the saintly transept altarpieces.

7 Enoteca I Terzi
MAP E4 ■ Via dei Termini 7
■ 057 744 329 ■ Open 11am–1am
Mon–Sat ■ www.enotecaiterzi.it

Located at the junction of the "thirds" which divides the town, this restaurant is housed in a 12th-century stone tower called "Torre dell'Orsa" or "dei Ballanti". Its interior features beautiful brick vaults and a cellar dug into tuff. The vast collection of wines here are available for purchase, and tastings can be organized as well.

8 Via Banchi di Sopra
MAP E4 ■ Via Banchi di Sopra

Siena's main *passeggiata* street is lined with palaces. Until Palazzo Pubblico was built, the city council met in the piazza between San Cristofano church and the 13th-century Palazzo Tolomei, now a bank. Up the street, Piazza Salimbeni is flanked by the Renaissance Palazzo Tantucci and Palazzo Spannocchi and the Gothic Palazzo Salimbeni. Together, this group of buildings houses Monte dei Paschi di Siena, the world's oldest bank (established 1472) and city's chief employer, and its small, worthy collection of Sienese paintings.

9 Casa di Santa Caterina
MAP E4 ■ Costa di
Sant'Antonio ■ Church: open
9am–12:30pm & 3–6pm daily

The house in which the saint was born was made a sanctuary in 1466, with a modest Baroque

San Domenico church

Frescoes, Casa di Santa Caterina

church containing the 12th-century Pisan Crucifixion that gave Catherine the stigmata, a brick loggia (built in 1533 by Baldassare Peruzzi) and a small oratory with Baroque paintings by Francesco Vanni, Il Riccio and Il Pomarancio. The stairs past her cell lead to the Oratorio dell'Oca.

Ledger cover detail, Archivio di Stato

(10) Archivio di Stato

Banchi di Sotto 52 ■ Open 10–11:30am Sat (reservations required for groups of 10 or more)

Siena's state archive (see p75) houses city accounts going back as far as 1258, which may not sound gripping, until you find out that the Sienese were in the habit of commissioning major local artists to decorate the cover of their annual accounts ledger. This unique collection of "Tavolette di Biccherna", housed in the archive museum, holds charming miniature masterpieces by Francesco di Giorgio and Beccafumi, among others.

A DAY IN SIENA

▶ MORNING

Start with the **Duomo** group (see p95), especially if it's winter, as the museum closes in the afternoon. Explore the Gothic nooks and Baroque crannies of the cathedral itself first, then pop across to **Santa Maria della Scala**. Don't skip the **Museo dell' Opera Metropolitana** (see p32) with works by Giovanni Pisano, Donatello and Duccio, plus fabulous views from the façade wall. Finally, descend the stairs to see the Baptistry before heading back around the other side of the Duomo for lunch at **Antica Osteria da Divo** (see p99). Skip dessert so that you can pick it up at the **Il Magnifico** pastry shop, located a short walk away at Via Stalloreggi 91–93, but don't eat it just yet.

AFTERNOON

Stroll back up Via Stalloreggi and Via di Città, where there are plenty of attractive shops, on your way to the **Piazza del Campo** (see p95). Either eat your Il Magnifico pastries or grab an outdoor table at **Bar Il Palio** (Piazza del Campo 47). Order a coffee or glass of wine, and drink in the ambience of one of the loveliest squares in Italy. Then head inside the **Palazzo Pubblico** (see p95) for the **Museo Civico** (see p36), which displays Siena's greatest Gothic art. Exit the Campo on the north side to join the locals for an espresso or Campari at the famed café **Nannini** (see p98) before joining the lively evening *passeggiata* (stroll) on Via Banchi di Sopra.

See map on pp94–5 ←

Shops, Cafés and Wine Bars

① Nannini
Via Banchi di Sopra 24
■ www.caffetterienannini.com
Siena's renowned premier café roasts its own coffee and serves delicious pastries.

② Ceramiche Artistiche Arcaico
Via di Città 92
■ 0577 287 873
■ Open 10am–7:30pm daily
Shop for Siena's best ceramics. The black, white and "burnt sienna" designs are modeled on the Duomo's floor panels.

Ceramiche Artistiche Santa Caterina

③ Trame di Storia
Via San Pietro 7
■ 0577 282 200 ■ Open 11:30am–6pm daily
Cinzia Gazzarri works her giant looms here, turning out colourful knitwear.

④ Cortecci
Il Campo 30–31 ■ Open 10am–7:30pm Mon–Sat ■ www.corteccisiena.it
Men's and women's designer fashion as well as some lesser-known, more affordable labels are on sale here.

Mannequin display at Cortecci

⑤ Antica Drogheria Manganelli
Via di Città 71–3 ■ Open 9:30am–7:30pm Mon–Sat ■ www.drogheriamanganelli.it
Speciality Sienese foods, such as wines, cheeses, preserves, salamis and biscuits, have been sold in this shop since 1879.

⑥ La Fabbrica delle Candele
Via dei Pellegrini 11 ■ Open 9:30am–7:30pm daily ■ www.lafabbricadellecandele.com
This pretty little shop just off Piazza Campo makes candles by hand in the *millefiori* tradition.

⑦ Manufactus
Via di Città 37 ■ Opening hours vary, check website ■ www.manufactus.it
A stationery store featuring marbled paper and leather-bound notebooks.

⑧ Compagnia dei Vinattieri
Via delle Terme 79 ■ 0577 236 568 ■ Open 12:30–2:45pm & 7:15–11pm daily
Innovative dishes are coupled with old favourites like *pici cacio e pepe* (pasta, *pecorino* and black pepper) at this tiny *enoteca*. The wines are excellent too.

⑨ Aloe & Wolf Gallery
Via del Porrione 23 ■ Open by appointment ■ www.aloewolf.it
This shop tucked behind Piazza del Campo sells vintage clothing and art.

⑩ Louis Ciocchetti
Via Banchi di Sopra 91
■ Open 10am–8pm daily ■ www.louisciocchetti.com
Jewellery, watches and Etruscan reproduction jewellery – all made in Italy – are available for sale here.

Restaurants

Diners at Osteria Le Logge

PRICE CATEGORIES

For a three-course meal for one with half a bottle of wine (or equivalent meal), taxes and extra charges.

€ under €35   €€ €35–70   €€€ over €70

1 Osteria Le Logge
Via del Porrione 33 ■ 057 748 013 ■ Closed Sun ■ €€

This ancient converted pharmacy offers the best traditional cuisine and friendliest service in town.

2 Antica Osteria da Divo
Via Franciosa 25/29 ■ 0577 286 054 ■ Closed Tue ■ €€

Medieval ambience, easy-going service and modern Tuscan cooking – including an Italian trend of pairing each main course with a side dish.

3 Osteria di Castelvecchio
Via di Castelvecchio 65 ■ 057 747 093 ■ Closed Wed (occasionally open for L) ■ €

The creative Tuscan food is quite refined for the price at this intimate little place. There is a daily selection of vegetarian meals.

4 Grotta di Santa Caterina "da Bagoga"
Via della Galluzza 26 ■ 0577 282 208 ■ Closed Sun D & Mon ■ €

Run by a former Palio jockey, this cellar-like restaurant specializes in traditional Sienese dishes such as stuffed chicken and wild boar stew.

5 Tre Cristi
Vicolo di Provenzano 1/7 ■ 0577 280 608 ■ Closed Sun ■ €€

A bastion of the Siena restaurant scene, this charming, traditional trattoria has a focus on fish.

6 Antica Trattoria Papei
Piazza del Mercato 6 ■ 0577 280 894 ■ €

Large, family-run trattoria serving solid Tuscan dishes under beamed ceilings or on the piazza outside. The restaurant also has a separate modernly furnished dining room.

7 Gino Cacino di Angelo
Piazza del Mercato 31 ■ 0577 223 076 ■ Open 8am–8pm daily ■ €

Sandwiches and cold cuts available to eat in or take away. The owner is extremely particular about sourcing the best local ingredients.

8 La Taverna del Capitano
Via del Capitano 6–8 ■ 0577 288 094 ■ €

A hand-scribbled menu of hearty dishes, with laid-back service and funky modern art.

9 La Sosta di Violante
Via Pantaneto 115 ■ 057 743 774 ■ Closed Sun ■ €

There is plenty of meat on the menu at this friendly, modern *osteria* named after a Bavarian princess. An extensive wine list complements the food.

10 Osteria La Chiacchera
Costa di Sant' Antonio 4 ■ 0577 280 631 ■ €

A remarkably budget-friendly restaurant with no cover charge. The *cucina povera* ("poor people's cuisine") and the great desserts change daily.

See map on pp94–5

TOP 10 Eastern Tuscany

Etruscan statue, Cortona

Arezzo province stretches from the thickly forested mountains of the Casentino in the north, down the northern arm of the Arno River valley, past the hamlet of Caprese where Michelangelo was born, to the wide Chiana Valley, the regional breadbasket. Aside from the happenstance of Michelangelo's birthplace, artistically the province is dominated by two early Renaissance titans: Sansepolcro's own Piero della Francesca in the province's northern half, and, in the south, the Cortona-born Luca Signorelli (1441–1523), whose fresco technique Michelangelo later studied avidly.

EASTERN TUSCANY

① **Top 10 Sights**
see pp103–5

① **Restaurants**
see p107

① **Shops and Cafés**
see p106

Heraldic shields at Arezzo's Piazza Grande

1 Arezzo

MAP F3 ■ Tourist office: Via Giorgio Vasari 13; 0575 377 678; www.discoverarezzo.com ■ San Francesco: Piazza S Francesco; 0575 352 727; open 9am–7pm Mon, Tue & Thu–Sat, 1–6pm Sun; adm

An Etruscan city and then a Roman pottery centre, Arezzo was home to Guido Monaco, inventor of modern musical notation; the poet Petrarch (1304–74), and Giorgio Vasari (1512–74), architect and author of *Lives of the Artists*. The Piazza Grande is the setting for the Giostra del Saracino jousting festival. The bell tower, façade and Calendar reliefs of the 12th-century Santa Maria della Pieve are in Lombard-Romanesque style, but the Pietro Lorenzetti altarpiece (1320) is Sienese Gothic. The Duomo has stained-glass windows by French master Guillaume de Marcillat, and a fresco by Piero della Francesca. San Francesco *(see p55)* is graced with Piero's fresco *Legend of the True Cross*.

2 Monte San Savino

MAP F4 ■ Tourist office: Piazza Gamurrini ■ 0575 849 418

This ceramics town has a small pottery museum, and the Santa Chiara church, with early works in terracotta by native sculptor Andrea Sansovino (1460–1529). He also carved marble (a sarcophagus in the Pieve), designed Sant'Agostino's loggias and cloisters and worked with Antonio da Sangallo the Elder on the Loggia dei Mercanti, opposite Sangallo's Palazzo di Monte.

3 Cortona

The quintessential Tuscan hill town *(see pp42–5)*, Cortona has medieval alleys, Renaissance art, Etruscan tombs and excellent restaurants.

4 Sansepolcro

MAP F3 ■ Tourist office: Via Matteotti 8 ■ Museo Civico: 10am–1pm & 2:30–6pm daily; www.museo civicosansepolcro.it

This medieval town has a reputation built around Piero della Francesca *(see p59)*. The Museo Civico *(see p56)* has Piero's famous *Madonna della Misericordia*, the *San Giuliano* fresco fragment and the compelling fresco *Resurrection of Christ*.

Detail, Piero's *Resurrection of Christ*

The hill town of Poppi

5 Poppi
MAP F3

The sweetest Casentino hill town, this is dominated by the Castello dei Conti Guidi (1274–1300), built by Lapo and Arnolfo di Cambio (also the architect of Florence's Palazzo Vecchio). Inside is a chapel, frescoed by 14th-century artist Taddeo Gaddi.

6 Lucignano
MAP F4

This tiny, elliptical town has a single street, which spirals to the lovely 16th-century Collegiata church. Behind the church, the Palazzo Comunale houses a museum with late Gothic Sienese paintings and a 2m- (6ft-) high gold reliquary dubbed *Tree of Lucignano* (1350–1471).

7 La Verna
MAP F3 ■ Santuario della Verna ■ 0575 5341 ■ Open 6:30–9:30am daily ■ www.laverna.it

St Francis himself founded this clifftop monastery. A Baroque frescoed corridor passes the now-enclosed cave where he slept. At the end of the corridor is the Cappella delle Stimmate, built over the site where the saint received his stigmata in 1224. For a sense of the saint's La Verna, unencumbered by buildings, walk to Sasso Spico, a rocky outcrop where the holy man prayed.

8 Camáldoli
MAP F2 ■ 52014 Camáldoli ■ 0575 556 021 ■ Pharmacy: open 9am–12:30pm & 2–6pm daily ■ www.camaldoli.it

San Romualdo established this Benedictine community in 1012, although the monastery is 15th century and the Vasari-decorated church 16th. 1.6 km (1 mile) up a forest path lies the secluded hermitage (only men are admitted), a tiny village of monkish cottages alongside a Baroque church.

9 Monterchi's Madonna del Parto
MAP F3 ■ Museo della Madonna del Parto, Via della Reglia 1; 0575 70 713; open 9am–1pm & 2–7pm daily; adm

Piero della Francesca's masterwork has the unusual subject of a heavily pregnant Virgin Mary, her tired face and drooping eyes revealed by

---

ST FRANCIS OF ASSISI

Son of a wealthy Assisi merchant, Francis (1182–1226) gave up his carousing, soldiering way of life after a crucifixion image spoke to him with an instruction to "rebuild my church". He renounced worldly goods, wrote a delightful set of poems and preached poverty and charity – the foundation of the Franciscan Orders. In 1224, while praying on La Verna, he received history's very first stigmata.

Monterchi's *Madonna del Parto*

angels pulling back the curtains. It was painted in a nearby chapel, where it became a focus of pilgrimage for pregnant women until it was moved to this small museum.

⑩ Castiglion Fiorentino
MAP F4 ■ Tourist info: Piazza Risorgimento 19 ■ 0575 658 278

Off the Piazza del Municipio and its lovely 1513 Vasari loggia stands the Pinacoteca. Housed in the former church of St Angelo, its trove of art includes the 13th-century *St Francis* by Margarito d'Arezzo, a fragment of Gaddi's *Maestà* (c.1328), as well as *St Francis Receiving the Stigmata* (c.1486) by Bartolomeo della Gatta.

Vasari loggia, Castiglion Fiorentino

A DAY IN AREZZO

▶ **MORNING**

Start at the **Museo Archeologico Mecenate** *(Via Margaritone 10)*, a museum of corallino pottery and other ancient artifacts that stands on a former Roman amphitheatre. Then head up Corso Italia to the **Piazza Grande** for coffee at one of the cafés under Vasari's loggia. Admire the square's Gothic and Renaissance *palazzi* before visiting the church of **Santa Maria della Pieve**. Then continue on Italia, and turn left onto Vicolo dell'Orto to climb up past the **Casa di Petrarca** (the poet's supposed house), then turn right onto Via Andrea Cesalpino to arrive at the **Duomo** and its masterful stained glass. Afterwards, stop by the tiny **Museo del Duomo** to see paintings by Tuscan artists Bartolomeo della Gatta and the father and son duo Spinello and Parri Aretino. Then go back downhill to lunch at **Vineria Ciao** *(see p107)*.

AFTERNOON

Having prebooked, head for the Piero works in **San Francesco** *(see p55)*. Return to Corso Italia to grab a gelato from **Cremi** *(see p106)*, then walk back down Via Cavour to the **Badia delle Sante Flora e Lucilla**. Above the altar note the trompe l'oeil "dome" (1702) painted by Baroque master of illusion Andrea Pozzo. Then walk down Via Garibaldi past SS Annunziata to the **Casa di Vasari** *(Via XX Settembre 55)*, home of historian and Medici court painter Giorgio Vasari. End at nearby **San Domenico** *(see p43)*, which has a Cimabue crucifix from the 1260s.

See map on p102

Shops and Cafés

1 Prada Outlet, Montevarchi
MAP E3 ▪ Levanella Via Aretina 403
▪ 0559 196 528 ▪ Open 10:30am–7:30pm daily

Arrive early in the day to avoid missing out on incredible deals on high fashion in this back-of-a-factory complex.

2 La Clandestina Cocktail & Food, Arezzo
MAP F3 ▪ Corso Italia 102 ▪ 0575 353 998 ▪ Open 6pm–1am daily

The lovely terrace and tasty cocktails are the main draw here.

3 Caffé degli Artisti, Cortona
MAP F4 ▪ Via Nazionale 18 ▪ 0575 601 237 ▪ Open 8am–11pm daily

Part locals' bar, part tourist shop selling honey, preserves, biscuits, meats, spices and olive oils.

4 L'Antico Cocciaio, Cortona
MAP F4 ▪ Via Benedetti 20
▪ 0575 605 294 ▪ Open 10:30am–1pm & 4:30–7:30pm Mon–Sat, 10:30am–1pm Sun

A lovely pottery shop selling ceramics in a palette of yellow, green and cream.

5 Enoteca Molesini, Cortona
MAP F4 ▪ Piazza della Repubblica 22/23 ▪ 0575 62 544 ▪ Open 9am–1:30pm & 4–8pm daily

Set on Cortona's main square, Enoteca Molesini offers good food and a great selection of wine.

6 Gelataria Artigianale Cremì, Arezzo
MAP F3 ▪ Corso Italia 100 ▪ 3393 869 544 ▪ Closed Mon

Central Arezzo's best natural gelato, offering creative and classic flavours.

Shoppers at Arezzo Antiques Market

7 Arezzo Antiques Fair
MAP F3 ▪ Piazza Grande
▪ Open 9am–8pm Sat (until 7pm Sun) 1st weekend of month ▪ www.fiera antiquaria.org

Over 600 antique dealers crowd the Piazza Grande and streets around it.

8 Di.Di.Gioielli, Arezzo
MAP F3 ▪ Via F Crispi 16
▪ 0575 26751 ▪ Open 9am–1pm & 3:30–8pm daily

This lovely jewellery store stocks pieces from Arezzo's famous manufacturer, Unoaerre.

Ceramic plate, L'Antico Cocciaio

9 Macelleria Aligi Barelli, Arezzo
MAP F3 ▪ Via della Chimera 22 ▪ 0575 357 754 ▪ Open 8am–1pm & 4:30–7:30pm Mon–Fri, Sat am only

A popular local butcher specializing in meats (mainly salami) from the Casentino region. This place is ideal for picnics.

10 Sottopiazza, Arezzo
MAP F3 ▪ Via di S Francesco 17

This cocktail bar on the historic Piazza S Francesco serves a variety of wines and spirits, with artisanal beer on tap.

Restaurants

1 Locanda dell'Amorosa, Amorosa

MAP F4 ■ Near Sinalunga ■ 0577 677 211 ■ www.amorosa.it ■ €€€

A 14th-century farm complex and inn, with a refined restaurant in the converted stalls. Classy Tuscan cuisine is served in a rustic, fire-warmed setting. Booking advised.

2 Il Falconiere, Cortona

MAP F4 ■ San Martino a Bocena 370 (just north of Cortona) ■ 0575 612 679 ■ €€€

The *limonaia* of Silvia and Riccardo Baracchi's 17th-century estate now houses this Michelin-starred restaurant, one of the finest in the region, adding rich flourishes to the already excellent Tuscan cuisine.

3 Vineria Ciao, Arezzo

MAP F3 ■ Via Giuseppe Garibaldi 15 ■ 0575 182 2174 ■ Closed Mon & D Sun ■ www.vineriadalchiodo.it ■ €

A charming family spot, this restaurant was built by carpenter Carlo (or Chiodo, as he's affectionately known). The menu offers satisfying Tuscan dishes cooked to perfection, with great wines to match.

4 Ristorante Fiorentino, Sansepolcro

MAP F3 ■ Via L Pacioli 60 ■ 0575 742 033 ■ Closed Wed ■ €

Old-fashioned inn *(see p73)* serving hearty, traditional food.

5 Preludio, Cortona

MAP F4 ■ Via Guelfa 11 ■ 0575 630 104 ■ €€

This gastronomic destination in Cortona serves nouvelle Tuscan dishes in a Renaissance palazzo setting (the frescoes are modern).

6 Il Forcillo, Sinalunga

MAP F4 ■ Viale Gramsci 7 ■ 0577 630 102 ■ €€

At this Tuscan *osteria,* annexed to a lovely hotel, there is a wide choice of local cuisine served by friendly staff. Try the ravioli with cheese and nettle.

7 Alo Burger, Arezzo

MAP F3 ■ Via Madonna del Prato 54 ■ 0575 350 660 ■ Closed Sun ■ €

If you're hankering for something quick, tasty and meaty, Alo Burger will hit the spot.

8 La Grotta, Cortona

MAP F4 ■ Piazza Baldelli 3 ■ 0575 630 271 ■ Closed Tue ■ €

Outdoor seating on a tiny piazza, stony medieval rooms and solid Tuscan dishes make this popular with locals and college students.

9 Antica Osteria l'Agania, Arezzo

MAP F3 ■ Via Mazzini 10 ■ 0575 300 205 ■ Closed Mon ■ €

Cosy trattoria where the comfort food includes *grifi e polenta* (fatty veal stomach in polenta).

10 La Loggetta, Cortona

MAP F4 ■ Piazza di Pescheria 3 ■ 0575 630 575 ■ Closed Wed ■ €€

Diners come here to enjoy the balcony setting and sample the delicious Tuscan cuisine made from quality local produce.

Outdoor seating area at La Loggetta

See map on p102

🔟 Northwestern Tuscany

The coastal northwestern corner of Tuscany is a land of craggy mountains, wide plains and beautiful Romanesque architecture. Proud, independent Lucca, with its bicycling grandmothers and exquisite Renaissance sculpture, managed to stay a Medici-free republic until Napoleon invaded. Lively university city Pisa retains its cultural heritage of the 11th to the 13th centuries, when its navy ruled the Western Mediterranean. Its magnificent medieval Piazza del Duomo is now a UNESCO World Heritage Site. Brash upstart Livorno has grown exponentially since the 16th century to become a major port. The three cities still nurse long-held bitter rivalries.

Bust of David, Carrara

NORTHWESTERN TUSCANY

1 Top 10 Sights
see pp109–11

1 Restaurants
see p113

1 Shops and Cafés
see p112

Pontrémoli **8**
Busana
Bagnone
Mulazzo
Tavernelle
Ligonchio
Aulla
Fivizzano
Sillano
Fosdinovo
Fantiscritti Marble Quarries
Sarzana
Carrara **5** **6** Colonnata **10**
Castiglione di Garfagnana
Cutigliano
La Lima
Bocca di Magra
Massa
Gallicano
Garfagnana Region **6**
Pontepetri
Borgo a Mozzano
Bagni di Lucca
Prunetta
Forte dei Marmi **9**
Pietrasanta
Camaiore
Marina di Pietrasanta
Pescia
Montecatini Terme **7**
Lido di Camaiore
Massarosa
Viareggio **4** **1** **5** **9** **10**
Lucca **2** **3** **9** **1** **3** **4** **6**
Vinci
Migliarino
San Giuliano Terme
Galleno
Fucecchio
Ligurian Sea
Pisa **1** **2** **7** **2**
Marina di Pisa
Pontedera
Ponte a Elsa
Calambrone
Vicarello
Ponsacco
Collesalvetti
Capannoli
Livorno **3**
Casciana Terme
La Sterza
Calafuria
Gabbro **10**

0 kilometres 15
0 miles 15

1 Pisa

A favourite day trip of visitors to Tuscany, this city *(see pp26–9)* offers more than just a leaning tower. Its gorgeous collection of Romanesque buildings called the Piazza del Duomo is among Tuscany's top sights.

2 Lucca

Another of the region's top sights, Lucca *(see pp46–7)* is a small, elegant city of avid cyclists, church concerts, Romanesque façades and exquisite Renaissance sculpture.

3 Livorno

MAP C3 ▪ Tourist office: Via Alessandro Pieroni 18/20; 0586 894 236 ▪ www.comune.livorno.it

Although Florence had already subjugated Pisa in the 16th century, Pisa's silty harbour and unsure loyalties prompted Cosimo I to hire Buontalenti to build him a new port from scratch. Livorno and Pisa have been traditional rivals ever since. Livorno is Tuscany's second city, but short on sights when compared with Pisa. There is just Pietro Tacca's Mannerist masterpiece *Monumento ai Quattro Mori* (1623–6) at the port, the somewhat wishfully named Venezia Nuova (New Venice) canal district, built by partly dismantling Buontalenti's Fortezza Nuova, and the Museo Civico Giovanni Fattori. The last is devoted to native son Fattori, one of the leading artists of the 19th-century Macchiaioli (Tuscan "Impressionists"). Artist Amedeo Modigliani was also born here (but worked in Paris), as was composer Pietro Mascagni.

Carnevale parade, Viareggio

4 Viareggio

MAP C2 ▪ Tourist office: Piazza Curtatone; 0583 442 213 ▪ www.turismo.lucca.it

Of all the Versilia beach resorts, Viareggio has the most style and substance. The Liberty style (Art Nouveau) of its many villas, cafés and buildings harks back to the resort's heyday in the 1920s. Its colourful Carnevale parade *(see p76)* has been taking place since 1873 and is renowned throughout both Italy and Europe.

Fortezza Nuova, Livorno

The Ponte del Diavolo spanning the Serchio in the Garfagnana

5 Carrara
MAP C2 ■ Tourist office: Piazza Alberica 10; 3358 343 272

Carrara is a quarry town, its snowy white marble the source of grandiose sculpture from ancient Rome to Michelangelo to Henry Moore. The town's Duomo is pure Carrara marble, and marble-cutting shops and sculptors' studios fill the streets. On the main square, the plaque and relief of stone-carving tools mark the house where Michelangelo once stayed. The Museo del Marmo features the ancient Roman altar Edicola di Fantiscritti.

6 Garfagnana Region
MAP C2–D2 ■ Piazza delle Erbe, Castelnuovo di Garfagnana

The Serchio River valley north of Lucca's plain (see p47) is bounded on the west by the Apuan Alps, which are home to the Grotta del Vento (Cave of the Winds). To the east are the wilds of the Garfagnana Mountains. Stop at Borgo a Mozzano, which consists of an inn and the Ponte del Diavolo bridge. Legend has it that this was built by the Devil in exchange for the first soul to cross it (villagers sent a dog). In the 19th century Bagni di Lucca was one of Europe's most fashionable spas, visited by all the English Romantic poets. Europe's first licensed public casino opened here in 1837. Barga's white Duomo has a marvellously detailed 13th-century pulpit carved by Guido da Como. The Este dukes once owned the 14th-century fortress of Castelnuovo di Garfagnana, and installed poet Ludovico Ariosto as commander and toll-taker.

7 Montecatini Terme
MAP D2 ■ Tourist office: Viale Verdi 66; 0572 772 244 ■ Baths: Viale Verdi 41; 0572 7781; www.termemontecatini.it ■ Monsummano Terme: Piazza IV Novembre 75; 0572 959 228

1930s Montecatini Terme poster

This posh thermal spa town (see p66) offers the experience of the 19th-century Grande Dame hotels. Above the town, medieval Montecatini Alto is a great escape for its cool summer breezes and a cappuccino on the piazza, while nearby Monsummano Terme (see p67) has natural cave saunas.

8 Pontrémoli
MAP B1 ■ Museum: Castello di Piagnaro; 0187 831 439; open 9:30am–5:30pm daily (Jun, Jul & Sep: until 6:30pm; Aug: until 7:30pm); adm

Stranded up a northern spit of Tuscany is Pontrémoli and its

Museo delle Statue-Stele. Some of the museum's 20-odd prehistoric menhirs (large upright stone slabs) date from 3000 BC, the more elaborate ones from 200 BC.

9 Forte dei Marmi

MAP C2 ■ Tourist office: **Via G. Carducci 6; 0584 280 253**

A tiny resort favoured by jet-setters, this village is set back amid the pine forest, its beach lined with colourful little beach cabanas.

10 Fantiscritti Marble Quarries

MAP C2 ■ Open 9am–dusk daily

Featured in the opening scenes of Bond film *Quantum of Solace*, these marble quarries make the Apuan Alps above Carrara appear snow-capped year round. Fantiscritti has a museum of traditional stonecutting tools, which can be reached by following the Carrione River to the Vara Bridge, a former rail link to the docks that was converted to road use in 1965.

Marble quarries at Fantiscritti

PISA AND LUCCA IN A DAY

▶ **MORNING**

Start your day at Pisa's iconic **Piazza del Duomo** *(see p109)*. Admire the Pisano pulpits in the **Duomo** *(see p54)* and the perfect acoustics of the Baptistry. Then pause to compare the artist's original sketches with reproductions of the finished frescoes displayed at the **Museo delle Sinopie** across the piazza. Admire the cathedral's treasures at the **Museo dell'Opera del Duomo** right by the **Leaning Tower**, where charts show how the Piazza buildings form various perfect geometries. Then head across the river to admire the stunning façade of Santa Maria della Spina, which is adorned with statues. Stroll along the Arno to the Ponte di Mezzo, turn right up Borgo Stretto then left into the colourful Vettovaglie Market to lunch at the **Trattoria Sant'Omobono** *(see p113)*.

AFTERNOON

Catch a train or drive to **Lucca** *(see pp46–7)*, where your first stop is the **Duomo** *(see p54)*. A 5-minute walk north will take you to **Torre Guinigi**, well worth climbing for the panoramas. Walk another few minutes north through **Piazza Anfiteatro** and under the glittering façade of **San Frediano** to see its *Miracles of San Frediano* frescoes and the shrunken body of St Zita, patron saint of maids and ladies-in-waiting. Retrace your steps to fashionable **Via Fillungo**, then walk south to the impressive **San Michele in Foro**. To end your day, head to the city walls. If you are staying the night, rent a bike to ride along the top of the walls (the shops close at 7:30pm but you can return it the next day); if not, stroll the walls on foot.

See map on p108 ←

Shops and Cafés

1 Buccellato Taddeucci, Lucca
MAP C2 ■ Piazza San Michele 34
Opened in 1881, this pastry shop is the oldest in Lucca. Treat yourself to its famed *Buccellato* – a traditional Lucchese cake made from a secret family recipe.

2 Caffè dell'Ussero, Pisa
MAP C3 ■ Lungarno Pacinotti 26
Look out over the Arno River and imbibe with the ghosts of Pisa's intellectual élite at one of Italy's oldest literary cafés, opened in 1794.

3 Carli, Lucca
MAP C2 ■ Via Fillungo 95
This atmospheric antique jewellers set under frescoed vaults dates from 1800 and also sells watches.

4 Enoteca Vanni, Lucca
MAP C2 ■ Piazza Salvatore 7
Lucca's best wine shop is guaranteed to raise the hairs on your neck, with its hundreds of bottles crowded into small cellar rooms.

5 Gran Caffè Margherita, Viareggio
MAP C2 ■ Viale Margherita 30
A late Art Nouveau building with Moorish influences, this historic bar is also a restaurant and is on Viareggio's main shopping street.

6 Forisportam, Lucca
MAP C2 ■ Piazza S Maria Bianca 2
This is another good shop for buying presents and souvenirs; you'll pay decent prices for highly decorated Renaissance-style ceramics from Montelupo and Deruta.

7 Gelateria La Gigia, Montecatini Alto
MAP D2 ■ Piazza G Giusti 27
Set in a pretty medieval town above Montecatini Terme, this small family-run gelateria serves excellent gelato and granita. Try their coffee with ice cream.

8 La Capannina, Forte dei Marmi
MAP C2 ■ Viale della Repubblica 16
Since 1929 La Capannina – part cocktail bar/restaurant and part nightclub – has been serving the best beachside refreshments around in this upmarket area.

9 Bar Galliano, Viareggio
MAP C2 ■ Viale Marconi 127
This historic café in the heart of the seaside promenade's shopping district is well known for its excellent ice creams, as well as great coffee, cakes and savoury snacks.

10 Rossi, Viareggio
MAP C2 ■ Viale Margherita 50
Rossi has been in the same family for five generations. In 1961 father Giuliano moved the shop to this prestigious location where they sell elegant pieces from the top names in Italian jewellery design for the discerning customer. It was the first jeweller and repair workshop in town.

Gran Caffè Margherita, Viareggio

Restaurants

Elegant interiors of Romano

PRICE CATEGORIES
For a three-course meal for one with half a bottle of wine (or equivalent meal), taxes and extra charges.

€ under €35   €€ €35–70   €€€ over €70

1 Romano, Viareggio
MAP C2 ■ Via Mazzini 120 ■ 0584 31 382 ■ Closed Mon, Jan, Tue L ■ €€€

Run by the Franceschini family, this is among the town's good seafood restaurants. Excellent wine list.

2 Trattoria Sant'Omobono, Pisa
MAP C3 ■ Piazza Sant'Omobono 6 ■ 050 540 847 ■ Closed Sun D ■ €

This classic trattoria (see p73) in the market area specializes in traditional Pisan cooking such as baccalà or salt cod and other seafood.

3 La Buca di Sant'Antonio, Lucca
MAP C2 ■ Via della Cervia 3 ■ 0583 55 881 ■ Closed Sun D, Mon ■ €

The ambience, classy but friendly service and superlative food make this (see p72) a great choice.

4 Antica Locanda di Sesto, near Lucca
MAP C2 ■ Via Ludovica 1660 ■ 0583 578 181 ■ Closed Sat ■ €€

This family-run inn (see p72) has been serving dishes made with fresh produce from their farm since the 1300s.

5 Extra, Carrara
MAP C2 ■ Viale Turigliano 13 ■ 0585 74 741 ■ Closed Sun ■ www.extracarrara.it ■ €€

Located in a glass and marble tower, Extra is a contemporary restaurant with an imaginative menu. Ask for a table on the sculpture-filled atrium overlooking the garden.

6 Venanzio, Colonnata, near Carrara
MAP C2 ■ Piazza Palestro 3 ■ 0585 758 033 ■ Closed Sun D, Thu & Christmas–mid-Jan ■ €€

Venanzio Vannucci produces his own lardo di Colonnata (herbed pork lard). Also try the ravioli with mountain herbs and guinea fowl with truffles.

7 Osteria dei Cavalieri, Pisa
MAP C3 ■ Via San Frediano 16 ■ 050 580 858 ■ Closed Sat L, Sun ■ €€

The beans and funghi (mushrooms) at this friendly tavern set in a medieval tower-house are a must-try.

8 Ristorante Butterfly, Marlia, near Lucca
MAP C2 ■ Via Del Brennero ■ 0583 307 573 ■ Closed Wed ■ €€€

A Michelin-starred restaurant, Butterfly offers creative Italian cuisine. During the summer visitors can dine in the garden.

9 Da Leo, Lucca
MAP C2 ■ Via Tegrimi 1 ■ 0583 492 236 ■ Closed Sun D ■ €

Da Leo is crowded with locals and buzzing with conversation. Try the zuppa ai cinque cereali, a soup filled with grains and legumes.

10 Il Romito, Livorno
MAP C3 ■ Via del Littorale 274 ■ 0586 580 520 ■ Closed Wed in winter ■ €€

With a spectacular clifftop setting and fresh fish on the menu, Il Romito (see p72) is a perfect stop for a meal.

See map on p108

TOP 10 Western Hill Towns

When people imagine the archetypal Tuscan hill town, they are most likely to be picturing those in the area west of Siena. This is where San Gimignano – one of Tuscany's seven UNESCO World Heritage Sites – thrusts its grey stone towers into blue skies, where Volterra's medieval streets and alabaster artisans sit atop "a towering great bluff that gets all the winds and sees all the world" (D H Lawrence). More off the beaten track, the underrated Elsa

Ceramic plate,
Massa Marittima

Valley is home to other attractive hill towns, including Colle di Val d'Elsa, Certaldo and Castelfiorentino, which have virtually no crowds and offer a better glimpse of genuine Tuscan town life.

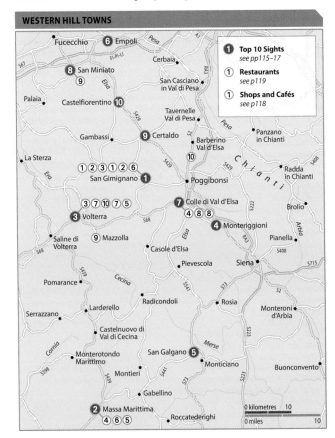

WESTERN HILL TOWNS

- **1** Top 10 Sights
  see pp115–17
- **1** Restaurants
  see p119
- **1** Shops and Cafés
  see p118

The charming medieval town of Volterra, surrounded by green hills

① San Gimignano

The ultimate hill town *(see pp24–5)* ranks second to none among Tuscany's most unmissable sights for its fine white wine, gorgeous Gothic frescoes and remarkable medieval stone "skyscrapers".

② Massa Marittima

MAP D4 ■ Tourist office: Piazza Garibaldi; 0566 906 554; www.turismo massamarittima.it ■ Museo San Pietro all'Orto: 0566 902 289; open summer: 9:30am–1pm & 2–6pm daily

This old mining town *(see p61)* has a number of esoteric museums on the subject. In the lower Old Town, the Dark Ages reliefs on the Romanesque Duomo *(see p54)* are worth a look. The Palazzo del Podestà, once the seat of the mayor, dates to the early 13th century. The upper New Town has the Gothic Torre del Candeliere and ramparts, with fine views over the town and Colline Metallifere (literally the "iron-rich hills"). The Museum of Sacred Art in the San Pietro all'Orto complex holds Ambrogio Lorenzetti's *Maestà* (1330s) and a tiny pre-Etruscan menhir, a flat stone carved vaguely as a person.

③ Volterra

MAP D4 ■ Tourist office: Piazza dei Priori 20; 058 887 257 ■ www.volterratur.it

Alabaster-carving is the speciality of this windswept town *(see p60)*. The Museo Etrusco Guarnacci *(see p57)* has one of Italy's finest Etruscan collections, and the worn basalt heads adorning Porta all'Arco (4th century BC) represent Etruscan gods. The remains of Roman baths and a theatre are best seen from the viewing point off Via Guarnacci. The Pisan-striped 13th-century Duomo, with its meticulously carved and painted ceiling, houses a host of Byzantine and Renaissance treasures, while the Pinacoteca features a fully intact Taddeo di Bartolo altarpiece (1411), Ghirlandaio's final painting *Apotheosis of Christ* (1492), Luca Signorelli's *Annunciation* (1491) and Rosso Fiorentino's masterful early Mannerist *Deposition* (1521).

④ Monteriggioni

MAP E4 ■ Tourist office: Piazza Roma; 0577 304 834

The subject of the most popular aerial-shot postcard in Tuscany is a tiny hamlet two streets wide. It is entirely enclosed within medieval walls, whose 14 towers were compared by Dante to the Titans guarding the lowest level of Hell. The town holds a week-long medieval festival in July.

An aerial look at Monteriggioni

Atmospheric San Galgano abbey

5 San Galgano
MAP E4 ■ Abbazia di S Galgano ■ Open 9am–8pm ■ Adm

This roofless 13th-century abbey and unique domed chapel on the hillside above are associated with the legend of a 12th-century soldier who plunged his sword into a stone (see p33) to mark the end of his warrior ways. Ambrogio Lorenzetti frescoes (1344) illustrate the holy vision that triggered the incident.

6 Empoli
MAP D3 ■ Tourist office: Via Giuseppe del Papa 41; 0571 757 622

Piazza Farinata degli Uberti is ringed by 12th- and 13th-century palaces and the Romanesque Sant'Andrea church. The Museo della Collegiata di Sant'Andrea contains a 1425 *Pietà* painted by Masolino da Panicale and a 1447 font carved by Bernardo Rossellino. Masolino shows up again at the church of Santo Stefano with a large *Madonna and Child* fresco; Rossellino with an *Annunciation*.

7 Colle di Val d'Elsa
MAP E3 ■ Tourist office: Via del Castello 33; 0577 922 791

Enter from the west to pass under Baccio d'Agnolo's Mannerist Palazzo Campana gate (1539). The Duomo features a Giambologna/Pietro Tacca bronze crucifix and a nail said to be from Christ's cross. The archaeological museum in the Palazzo Pretorio shows 1920s political graffiti scrawled on this former prison's walls by imprisoned Communists. The sgraffito-covered façade of Palazzo dei Priori hides a museum of Sienese paintings.

8 San Miniato
MAP D3 ■ Tourist office: Piazza del Popolo 1; 057 142 233

Frederick II built the imposing hilltop "Rocca" (fortress) when this was the Tuscan stronghold of the German Holy Roman Emperors. The Duomo's (rebuilt) Romanesque brick façade is studded with 13th-century North African majolica bowls.

9 Certaldo
MAP D3 ■ Tourist office: Via Giovanni Boccaccio 16; 0571 652 730

In this charming little brick town, Renaissance artists Benozzo Gozzoli and Giusto d'Andrea teamed up to work on the *Giustiziati* tabernacle in the former church of SS Thomas e Prospero, which is now part of the Palazzo Pretorio museum complex.

Piazza Farinata degli Uberti in Empoli

Frescoes, Palazzo Pretorio, Certaldo

Inside SS Michele e Jacopo church, a 1503 bust and 1954 tombstone commemorate *Decameron* author Boccaccio (1313–75), who may have been born in Certaldo; the Casa del Boccaccio, in which he passed his final years, is now a small museum.

⑩ Castelfiorentino

MAP D3 ■ Tourist office: Via Ridolfi 13; 0571 629 049 ■ Santa Verdiana Museo: open 9am–1pm & 3–7pm Mon–Fri

Santa Verdiana is the loveliest and most celebrated Baroque church in Tuscany. Its interior is swathed in frescoes depicting the odd life of Verdiana, who walled herself into a cell here for 34 years with two snakes, said to be sent by God to test her.

DANTE

Dante Alighieri (1265–1321) was Florence's White Guelph (papal) diplomat to San Gimignano. Exiled from Florence on trumped-up charges when the Black Guelphs took over, Dante roamed Italy writing poetry, including the epic *Divine Comedy*. His choice of writing in Tuscan vernacular rather than Latin legitimized and codified the Italian language.

A DAY IN THE HILL TOWNS

▶ MORNING

Begin early in the morning in **Volterra** *(see p115)*, starting with San Francesco and its amazing *Legend of the True Cross* frescoes. On the Piazza dei Priori, admire the Palazzo dei Priori (1208–57) inside and out. It is the oldest Gothic town hall in Tuscany and was the model for most others, including Florence's Palazzo Vecchio. Tucked into an alcove on the square is the back door of the Duomo – dive inside. Afterwards, pause for coffee and a pastry at L'Incontro *(see p118)*, then head back to the piazza and down Via dei Sarti to the Pinacoteca and Fiorentino's *Deposition (see p58)*, a Florentine Mannerist masterpiece. The museum is usually blissfully quiet. Continue on this street into Via di Sotto, which is lined with good alabaster workshops, then to Via Don Minzoni for the Museo Etrusco Guarnacci *(see p57)*.

AFTERNOON

Drive 8 km (5 miles) to the pretty hamlet of **Mazzolla** for a rustic lunch at the **Trattoria Albana** *(see p119)* before driving another 28 km (17 miles) to **San Gimignano** *(see pp24–5)*. You should get there just as the tour buses are leaving (but before 4pm in winter, when things close early). Admire the Collegiata frescoes before clambering up the Torre Grossa for one of Tuscany's most beautiful panoramas over the surrounding hills and vineyards. If you have time after descending – and after pausing at the Museo Civico – head to the other end of town for Sant'Agostino's Benozzo Gozzoli frescoes (before 6:30pm). Try to be back up at the ruined Rocca for sunset over the towers.

See map on p114 ←

Shops and Cafés

Gelato and sorbet at the Gelateria "di Piazza", San Gimignano

1 Gelateria Dondoli, San Gimignano
MAP D3 ■ Piazza della Cisterna 4
■ www.gelateriadondoli.com

The best gelato and sorbet in town, with unusual flavours such as pink grapefruit and sparkling wine on offer.

2 Souvenir Shops, San Gimignano
MAP D3 ■ Via S Giovanni

Souvenir shops line Via S Giovanni, selling medieval-style crossbows, swords and flails of varying types.

3 Società Cooperativa Artieri Alabastro, Volterra
MAP D4 ■ Piazza dei Priori 5
■ www.artierialabastro.it

Since 1895 this has been the main outlet for alabaster artisans without a shop of their own.

4 Manufactum, Colle Val d'Elsa
MAP E3 ■ Via del Castello 32
■ www.manufactum.it

Colourful Tuscan ceramics made and hand-painted in the shop.

5 Enoteca Le Logge, Massa Marittima
MAP D4 ■ Piazza Garibaldi 11
■ 0566 914 345

Great, simple Old World café with tables set under the partly frescoed portico of the piazza; their gelato and sandwiches are worth a try.

6 D! Vineria, San Gimignano
MAP D3 ■ Piazza delle Erbe 1
■ www.divineria.it

This wine bar has a tiny, but amazing terrace and a great wine selection. Snacks are also available.

7 L'Incontro, Volterra
MAP D4 ■ Via Matteotti 18
■ 0588 80 500 ■ Closed Wed

A lovely pastry and panini wine bar occupying an airy vaulted medieval room. Artisan gelato is sold out front.

8 Belli, Colle Val d'Elsa
MAP E3 ■ Via Diaz 12–14
■ 0577 926 749

The Etruscans once crafted crystal in this area. Belli carries on the tradition, producing both refined objects and souvenirs.

9 Il Cantuccio di Federigo, San Miniato
MAP D3 ■ Via P Maioli 67 ■ 0571 418 344 ■ Closed D Sun

The Gazzarrinis have been making pastries, cakes and biscuits for five generations. To go with their *cantucci* they carry over 40 Vin Santo labels.

10 Spartaco Montagnani, Volterra
MAP D4 ■ Via Porta all'Arco 6
■ 0588 86 184

A local sculptor's shop featuring his original bronzes as well as replicas of works in the museum.

Restaurants

① Dorandò, San Gimignano
MAP D3 ▪ Vicolo dell'Oro 2
▪ 0577 941 862 ▪ Closed Mon ▪ €€

Crisp tablecloths and excellent service are coupled with fascinating menus explaining the origins of each finely prepared dish at this cosy restaurant *(see p72)*.

② Osteria delle Catene, San Gimignano
MAP D3 ▪ Via Mainardi 18 ▪ 0577 574 998 ▪ Closed Wed, Oct–Mar: Sun D ▪ €€

Dine in a softly lit brick-barrelled vault at this *osteria* which offers great platters of cheeses and cured meats, along with a good selection of wines.

③ La Mangiatoia, San Gimignano
MAP D3 ▪ Via Mainardi 5 ▪ 0577 941 094 ▪ Closed Tue ▪ €€

The more imaginative dishes at "The Trough" are excellent (though the standard fare is not as impressive). Classical music adds to the lively atmosphere.

④ La Tana dei Brilli, Massa Marittima
MAP D4 ▪ Vicolo Ciambellano 4
▪ 0566 901 274 ▪ Closed Wed ▪ €€

Italy's smallest Slow Food *osteria* is big on rustic charm. Dishes are rooted in the Maremma, and are prepared using ingredients such as chestnut flour and wild boar.

⑤ Trattoria del Sacco Fiorentino, Volterra
MAP D4 ▪ Via Giusto Turazza 13
▪ 0588 88 537 ▪ Closed Wed ▪ €€

Enjoy superb wines and traditional seasonal specialities at this cosy central trattoria.

⑥ Taverna del Vecchio Borgo, Massa Marittima
MAP D4 ▪ Via Norma Parenti 12
▪ 0566 903 950 ▪ Closed D & Mon ▪ €€

Try the *tris di primi* sampler of three first courses at this friendly restaurant, located in an atmospheric cellar.

⑦ Del Duca, Volterra
MAP D4 ▪ Via di Castello 2
▪ 0588 81 510 ▪ Closed Tue ▪ €€

Family-run restaurant specializing in historic Volterran cooking, overseen by convivial chef-owner Genuino.

The family-run Del Duca restaurant

⑧ Arnolfo, Colle di Val d'Elsa
MAP E3 ▪ Via XX Settembre 50–52a
▪ 0577 920 549 ▪ Closed Tue & Wed ▪ €€€

This two-starred Michelin restaurant, set in a 15th-century palazzo, offers refined cooking as well as wines. Try to grab a table on the scenic terrace.

⑨ Trattoria Albana, near Volterra
MAP D4 ▪ Via Comunale 69 Loc., Mazzolla ▪ 0588 39 001 ▪ €

This traditional trattoria appeared in BBC's *Trip to Italy* series. Try the signature dish, ravioli with guinea fowl.

⑩ La Sosta di Pio VII, Barberino Val d'Elsa
MAP E3 ▪ Località Sosta del Papa
▪ 055 807 5923 ▪ €

Simple dishes like pasta with rabbit *ragù* and *tagliata* (steak) with bitter radicchio let the ingredients sing.

See map on p114 ←

🔟 Southern Tuscany

Montalcino
enoteca **sign**

If ever Bacchus blessed a landscape, it was the hilly terrain south of Siena. The dry clay soil is ideal for those Mediterranean plants: grapevines and olive trees. Two of Italy's mightiest red wines hail from these parts – Brunello di Montalcino and Vino Nobile di Montepulciano. And where even the vines can't take hold, grasslands thrive to provide rich grazing for sheep on the hills around Pienza, their milk producing the finest *pecorino* cheeses. Charming medieval hill towns, cypress-lined roads, isolated monasteries, Renaissance *palazzi*, Sienese School altarpieces and Etruscan tombs complete the picture.

Montepulciano

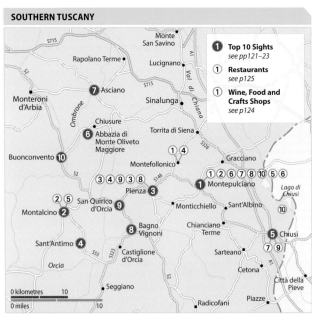

SOUTHERN TUSCANY

① **Top 10 Sights**
see pp121–23

① **Restaurants**
see p125

① **Wine, Food and Crafts Shops**
see p124

1 Montepulciano
MAP F4 ▪ Tourist office: Piazza
Don Minzoni 1; 0578 757 341
▪ www.prolocomontepulciano.it

This hill town *(see p61)* features
buildings by major Renaissance
architects and Tuscany's second
greatest wine, Vino Nobile *(see p71)*.
Via Gracciano nel Corso is lined with
Renaissance *palazzi* by the likes of
Vignola and Antonio da Sangallo the
Elder. Also look out for Palazzo Bucelli
(No. 73), its base embedded with
Etruscan urns. The Piazza Grande
is flanked by palaces by Sangallo,
the town's Duomo and the Palazzo
Comunale, which is Michelozzo's
tribute to Florence's Palazzo Vecchio.
Inside the Duomo are Michelozzo
sculptures that once formed a single
tomb, while the gilded altarpiece is
Taddeo di Bartolo's Sienese Gothic
masterpiece of 1401. Set on a patch
of grass below the town walls is
Sangallo's geometrically precise
church of Tempio di San Biagio
(1518–34), the best example of the
High Renaissance trend towards
Greek Cross churches.

2 Montalcino
MAP E4 ▪ Tourist office:
Piazza del Popolo; 0577 849 331
▪ www.montalcino.net

The hometown *(see p61)* of Brunello
(see p71), Tuscany's mightiest wine, is
a small but proud burg, with an excellent wine shop in the 14th-century
fortezza (see p124), a split-level main
square and a 1292 tower. The Museo
Civico e Diocesano houses paintings
by Simone Martini, Sano di Pietro and
Vecchietta, and polychrome wood
statues by Francesco di Valdambrino.

The abbey of Sant'Antimo

Wheels of cheese for sale, Pienza

3 Pienza
MAP F4 ▪ Tourist office: Via
delle Case Nuove 4; 366 248 6015
▪ Duomo: Piazza Pio II; open daily

This assemblage of buildings is a
UNESCO World Heritage Site, and
includes a retro-Gothic town hall,
a bishop's palace (now the Museo
Diocesano with art by Bartolo di
Fredi, Pietro Lorenzetti, Vecchietta
and), a papal palace with great
hanging gardens and a Duomo
(see p55). Corso Rossellino, the
town's main street, is packed
with wine and cheese shops.

4 Sant'Antimo
MAP E5 ▪ Abbazia di
Sant'Antimo: open 10am–
6:30pm daily

A French-style Romanesque
abbey *(see p54)* church standing
in a countryside setting. Concerts
and spiritual workshops are also
held here.

Porsenna labyrinth tunnels, Chiusi

5 Chiusi

MAP F5 ■ Tourist office: Via Porsenna 79; 0578 227 667 ■ www. prolocochiusi.it/en

Chiusi's fine Museo Archeologico Nazionale Etrusco contains *bucchero* (black Etruscan earthenware), a few 2nd-century-BC painted funerary urns, bronzes and Canopic jars. Buy tickets to visit the Etruscan tombs in the valley, including the Tombs of the Lion, the Pilgrim and the Monkey. The 12th-century Duomo is covered in trompe l'oeil frescoes (1887–94) that look like medieval mosaics. The adjacent Museo della Cattedrale preserves 15th-century illuminated scores from the Abbazia di Monte Oliveto Maggiore. Meet here for guided visits to the tunnels of the Etruscan Labirinto di Porsenna.

6 Abbazia di Monte Oliveto Maggiore

MAP E4 ■ Monte Oliveto Maggiore ■ 0577 707 258 ■ Open 9:30am–12:20pm & 2:30–4:40pm daily (summer: until 5:40pm)

On a hilltop in the Crete Senesi landscape of eroded clay and limestone bluffs is a 1313 Benedictine monastery (see p75). Its cloister is frescoed with the *Life of St Benedict*, a masterpiece of High Renaissance narrative painting by Signorelli (the west wall's eight scenes; 1497–8) and Sodoma (the other 25 scenes; 1505–8). Sodoma inserted a self-portrait in the third scene, his pet badgers at his feet.

7 Asciano

MAP E4 ■ Tourist office: Via Amos Cassioli 2 ■ www. prolocoasciano.it

With 14th-century walls and a travertine Romanesque Collegiata, Asciano stands amid the photogenic Crete Senesi hills. Palazzo Corboli, decorated with 14th-century civic frescoes, holds the town's archae-ological and sacred art collections, with panels by Ambrogio Lorenzetti and others. The Cassioli Museum is the only museum in Siena province dedicated to art from the Sienese School of the 19th century.

8 Bagno Vignoni

MAP E5

Little more than houses around a vast, Medici-built portico and basin steaming with naturally carbonated, volcanically heated waters. Lorenzo the Magnificent and St Catherine both bathed here, but sadly the old basin is no longer in use. Today the thermal baths are run by the town-ship and offer a range of therapies.

The old basin at Bagno Vignoni

Collegiata carving, San Quirico

(9) San Quirico d'Orcia
MAP E4 ■ Tourist office: Via
Dante Alighieri 33; 0577 899 728

A friendly little farming town that
has amazing Romanesque carvings
on the Collegiata's trio of 12th-century
portals. Spot many fantastical crea-
tures, stacked arches, tiny telamons
and thin columns "knotted" in the
centre and resting on toothless lions.
Inside is a Sano di Pietro altarpiece.

(10) Buonconvento
MAP E4 ■ Tourist office
(at the museum): Piazzale Garibaldi;
0577 809 744; www.prolocobuon
convento.com

The tiny historic centre shelters a
good Museo d'Arte Sacra, holding
Sienese School works by Duccio,
Sano di Pietro and Matteo di
Giovanni, who also left a *Madonna
and Child* in the town's 14th-century
Santi Piero e Paolo church.

A DAY'S DRIVE

▶ MORNING

Start at 9am in **Chiusi**, at the
Museo Archeologico Nazionale
Etrusco. After learning about the
Etruscans, head across the piazza
to join a Labirinto di Porsenna
tour. They leave every 40 minutes,
so you might be able to squeeze
in a 10-minute tour of the Museo
della Cattedrale as well. Then
retrieve your car and take the
winding S146 to **Montepulciano**
(see p121). Park at the base of
town to stroll up Via Gracciano
nel Corso (its name changes
constantly), sampling wines along
the way. Stop for lunch at the
Liberty-style Caffè Poliziano *(Via
Voltaio nel Corso 27–29)*, which
has served light meals with great
countryside views since 1858.

AFTERNOON

After lunch, continue up the main
street and pop inside the Gesù to
admire Andrea Pozzo's illusionary
painted "dome". Next head to the
Piazza Grande (more wine shops)
and then on to the Duomo. Then
drive on to **Pienza** *(see p121)* but
just before hitting the S146, stop
at Via dei Canneti at the edge of
Montepulciano to see the Tempio
di San Biagio (you can skip the
bare interior). Pienza is a quick
stop. After viewing the Duomo's
altarpieces *(see p55)* and the giant
cracks from the settling of the
cliff, tour Pope Pius II's Palazzo
Piccolomini. An alley next to the
palazzo leads to Via Gozzante, a
panoramic walkway out of town.
Drive on to **Montalcino** *(see p121)*.
In summer, head to the fortress
for sunset views from the ramparts; in winter, make your way to
the historic Caffè Fiaschetteria
Italiana in the main square.

See map on p120 →

Wine, Food and Crafts Shops

Barrels of wine at Contucci

1 Contucci, Montepulciano
MAP F4 ■ Via del Teatro 1
■ 0578 757 006

These winemaker's labyrinthine cellars are inside a Renaissance palazzo. The range includes Vino Nobile DOCG wines and a sweet Vin Santo.

2 Gattavecchi, Montepulciano
MAP F4 ■ Via Collazzi 74 ■ Open 11am–5pm ■ Closed Wed

Leading winery (see p70) with grotto-like cellars. It sells Vino Nobile wines as well as estate olive oil. There is a small tasting fee.

3 La Bottega del Naturista, Pienza
MAP F4 ■ Corso Rossellino 16 ■ Open 9am–1pm & 3–7pm daily

Boutique with every kind of *pecorino* plus honey, pâtés and conserves.

4 Biagiotti & Figli, Pienza
MAP F4 ■ Corso Il Rossellino, 67 ■ www.biagiottipienza.com/en

Cast and wrought iron of great beauty in everything from bedsteads

and candlesticks to fantastical chandeliers, all handmade the traditional way using hammer and anvil.

5 Enoteca La Fortezza, Montalcino
MAP E4 ■ Piazzale Fortezza ■ Open 9am–8pm daily

Enjoy the best selection of wine (and other goods) in the gorgeous remains of the town's medieval fortress.

6 Aliseda, Montepulciano
MAP F4 ■ Via dell'Opio nel Corso 8 ■ 0578 758 672

Unique but expensive gold jewellery, inspired by ancient museum pieces.

7 Maledetti Toscani, Montepulciano
MAP F4 ■ Vicolo di Voltaia 40 ■ Open 10:30am–7pm daily

A bit of everything handcrafted and Tuscan: leatherwork, wrought iron, copper pots and more.

8 Bottega del Rame, Montepulciano
MAP F4 ■ Via dell'Opio nel Corso 64 ■ Open 10am–7pm daily

The Mazzetti family sells a range of beautiful hand-hammered copperware.

9 Enoteca di Ghino, Pienza
MAP F4 ■ Via del Leone 16 ■ Open 9am–1pm & 2:30–7:30pm ■ Closed Wed in winter

Copper grapes, Bottega del Rame

One of Tuscany's best wine shops, with a good selection at almost every price.

10 Legatoria Koiné, Montepulciano
MAP F4 ■ Via Gracciano nel Corso 22 ■ Open 10am–7pm Mon–Sat

Beautiful leather-bound books and albums, each individually crafted in their *bottega* using the best-quality vegetable-tanned leather.

Restaurants

1 La Chiusa, Montefollonico

MAP F4 ■ Via della Madonnina 88 (near Montepulciano/Pienza) ■ 0577 669 668 ■ Closed Tue ■ €€€

Set in an 18th-century oil mill, La Chiusa serves creative Tuscan cooking using local, seasonal ingredients.

2 Ristorante Il Giglio Montalcino

MAP E4 ■ Via Soccorso Saloni 5 ■ 0577 848 167 ■ Closed Tue ■ €€€

A refined restaurant located in the hill town of Montalcino in Siena. It is known for its innovative cuisine as well as excellent wine cellar. Booking advised.

3 Trattoria Latte di Luna, Pienza

MAP F4 ■ Via San Carlo 2–4 ■ 0578 748 606 ■ €

Enjoy simple, soulful southern Tuscan cooking alfresco. Try the *pici* with garlic tomatoes or the roast suckling pig.

4 La Botte Piena, near Montefollonico

MAP F4 ■ Piazza Cinughi 12, Torrita di Siena ■ 0577 669 481 ■ Closed Wed, Thu L ■ €€

Oak-beamed ceiling, stone and brick walls and food steeped in the traditions of the Sienese countryside.

5 Acquacheta, Montepulciano

MAP F4 ■ Via del Teatro 22 ■ 0578 717 086 ■ Closed Tue ■ €

This place is a shrine to steaks (*bistecca*) which are ordered by weight before being brought to the table for approval. They are then briefly cooked on the flamegrill. Tasty sides include baked *pecorino* cheese with pear.

6 Ristorante La Grotta, Montepulciano

MAP F4 ■ Via San Biagio 15 ■ 0578 757 479 ■ Closed Wed ■ €€

Top-class Tuscan cuisine is created in this beautiful Renaissance building with vaulted terracotta ceilings. The service is impeccable.

Tuscan *ribollita* soup with bread

7 Ristorante Bar Il Bucchero, Chiusi

MAP F5 ■ Via Bonci 28 ■ 0578 222 092 ■ Closed Wed ■ €

Casual trattoria with home-style cooking. Try the ravioli, pici or tagliatelle smothered in porcini mushrooms and earthy truffles

8 Osteria Sette di Vino, Pienza

MAP F4 ■ Piazza di Spagna 1 ■ 0578 749 092 ■ Closed Wed ■ €

Tiny *osteria* with great mixed platters of *pecorino* cheese and salamis and a secret-family-recipe salad dressing.

9 La Solita Zuppa, Chiusi

MAP F5 ■ Via Porsenna 21 ■ 0578 21 006 ■ Closed Tue ■ €

A cosy spot offering traditional southern Tuscan dishes such as *pici* with duck sauce and Florentine trippa.

10 Ristorante Pesce D'Oro, Lago di Chiusi

MAP F4 ■ Località Sbarchino 36 ■ 0578 21 403 ■ Closed Tue ■ €

Set close to Chiusi's tranquil lake, which provides the fresh catch of the day, this restaurant offers a solid fish menu and a good wine selection.

See map on p120

🔟 The Southern Coast and Maremma

This is Tuscany's undiscovered corner, a largely flat area with a few low hills capped by crumbling ancient hill towns such as Pitigliano and Sorano. Its overgrown valleys hide Etruscan tombs, altars and sunken roads. This was the heart of Etruria, a fertile breadbasket and home to important Etruscan cities. But the conquering Romans were not as adept at maintaining large-scale drainage and irrigation systems, and this agricultural paradise quickly reverted to malarial swampland. The population dwindled, the ancient cities crumbled and most Tuscan powers left the Maremma alone. It was not until 1828 that Grand Duke Leopold I started draining the land again. Today, it is Tuscany's least disturbed repository of Etruscan heritage, while also offering beaches, Tuscany's best natural park and the Tyrrhenian islands.

A view of Pitigliano

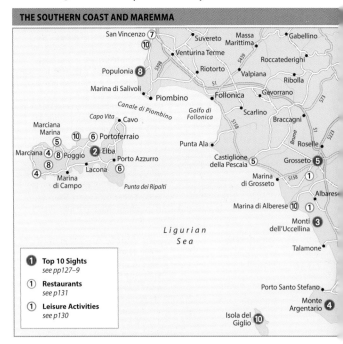

THE SOUTHERN COAST AND MAREMMA

1 **Top 10 Sights**
see pp127–9

1 **Restaurants**
see p131

1 **Leisure Activities**
see p130

1 Pitigliano

MAP F6 ■ Tourist office: Piazza Garibaldi; 0564 617 111 ■ www. comune.pitigliano.gr.it

Etruscan Pitigliano (see p61) seems to grow right out of its rocky terrain. This hill town's greatest sight is its medieval self, though the Palazzo Orsini castle (a 13th-century structure, enlarged by Giuliano da Sangallo) houses – apart from its own rooms – a few modest museums of local Etruscan finds, including the Museo Civico Archeologico. The synagogue offers tours of Pitigliano's tiny, labyrinthine Jewish ghetto, which all but vanished after Nazi deportations.

2 Elba

MAP C5 ■ Tourist office: Via Vittorio Emanuele II 2, Portoferraio; 0565 193 3589 ■ www.visitelba.info

This modestly scaled resort island (see p67), with its great beaches, derives its name from Aethalia, the

Cavoli beach on the island of Elba

Greek word for the sparks of its busy iron forges. Portoferraio, where ferries arrive from Piombino, has three forts, Napoleon's Villa dei Mulini (his Villa San Martino south of town is more interesting, however), and a small archaeological museum. Porto Azzuro was the island's Spanish capital and is today a bustling resort that retains something of the old fishing town. Hilltop Capoliveri has the best nightlife and evocative medieval alleyways. Marciana is a good hill town base for exploring the island's western half.

3 Monti dell'Uccellina

MAP E6 ■ Park entrance at Alberese ■ 0564 393 238 ■ Open 7:30am–dusk daily (Oct–mid-Jun: 9am–dusk) ■ Adm ■ www.parco-maremma.it

The greatest protected parkland in Tuscany, coastal Monti dell'Uccellina ("Mountains of the Little Bird") is a large area of pine forests teeming with boar, roe deer and porcupines, bird-filled marshland to the north and tracts of pristine beach. A pack of wild horses and roaming long-horned white Maremma cattle are looked after by Butteri cowboys. Buses from Albarese take you to the centre of the park.

4 Monte Argentario

MAP E6 ■ Tourist office: Piazzale del Valle, Porto Santo Stefano ■ 0564 332 075 ■ www. monteargentario.info

This quietly chic and beautiful peninsula (see p67) is really an almost-circular island, connected to the Tuscan mainland by causeways.

5 Grosseto

MAP E5 ■ Tourist office: Via Grossetana 206; 0564 36 306 ■ www.comune.grosseto.it

Grubby Grosseto lacks real charm, but Museo Civico Archeologico e d'Arte della Maremma showcases superb Etruscan artifacts. Many of the more portable finds from the Maremma are housed here, along with works of art from city churches, including Guido da Siena's 13th-century *Last Judgement* and a Sassetta *Madonna of the Cherries*. The 13th-century church of San Francesco has fresco fragments and a high altar *Crucifix* (1285) attributed to Duccio.

The Duomo of Sovana

6 Sovana

MAP F6

This modest hamlet was once an Etruscan city, Roman *municipium*, and birthplace of 11th-century Aldobrandeschi Pope Gregory VII, who reigned for 12 years. On the main square are a medieval Palazzo Pretorio and the church of Santa Maria, which contains 15th-century frescoes and a rare 9th-century altar canopy. Built between the 8th and 13th centuries, the Duomo on the edge of town preserves carvings from the Dark Ages. The surrounding hills and valley have signposted Etruscan tombs (see p68), altars and *vie cave*; the best is the Tomba Ildebranda.

7 Saturnia

MAP E6 ■ Spa: 0564 600 111; www.termedisaturnia.it

Visitors come to Saturnia not for the little town and its 15th-century

---

THE VIE CAVE

No one is sure why the Etruscans dug these "sunken roads", narrow canyons up to 20 m (65 ft) deep into the rocky ground of the Maremma. Many extend for kilometres between settlements. They may have been defensive, religious (some led to tombs or altars), for herding or perhaps some mixture of all these possibilities.

Sienese castle but to relax in the town's beautiful pools. The valley's warm, mineral-rich waters feed an elegant, four-star spa (see p66), a hotel and the lovely Cascate del Mulino, which gushes down a hillside, running into small thermal pools and waterfalls.

8 Populonia

MAP C5 ■ Baratti ■ 056 652 012 ■ Necropolis: opening hours vary, check website ■ Adm ■ www. parchivaldicornia.it

Baratti Bay's Iron Age role as port for Elba's mines helped preserve Populonia's Etruscan necropolis – under a slag heap. Half a dozen of the tombs are visitable to the public and several are almost intact. Museo Gasparri holds many of the interesting items excavated here, including bronze ornaments and funerary objects.

Isola del Giglio

The ancient hill town of Sorano

9 Sorano

MAP F5 ■ Tourist office:
Piazza Busati; 0564 633 099
■ www.comune.sorano.gr.it

Sorano is an ancient Etruscan hill town literally slipping off its rocky outcrop. The restored 11th-century Aldobrandeschi fortress (expanded by the Orsini in 1552) is now part medieval museum, part small hotel (see p143). The town's 18th-century Massa Leopoldino fortress is also open to visitors.

10 Isola del Giglio

MAP D6 ■ Tourist office:
Via Provinciale 9; 0564 809 400
■ www.isoladelgiglio.it

This hilly isle off l'Argentario (ferries from Porto Santo Stefano) has the medieval hamlet of Castello above the docks, a beach at the port and an even better low-key resort and beach on the bay at Campese. Ansonico, the local wine, is known mainly to the habitués who crowd here on summer weekends.

THE BEST OF THE MAREMMA IN A DAY

▶ **MORNING**

Begin your day in **Saturnia**. Skip the spa and head to the **Cascate del Mulino** (see p66) open-air hot springs south of town, where you can wallow in the wonderful natural whirlpools for free.

After the mineral soak, drive east towards Sovana. Look for signs indicating Etruscan ruins (tomba, ipogeo) and semi-subterranean paths cut through the soft volcanic tufa rock (vie cave). Explore as many as you can – especially the spectacular Tomba Ildebranda – before heading into **La Taverna Etrusca** (see p131) in **Sovana** for lunch. Pop into Santa Maria church and the Duomo, which preserves good carvings, some predating the Romanesque era.

AFTERNOON

Continue east to **Sorano** to visit the Fortezza degli Orsini (it reopens for the afternoon at 4pm), an 11th-century fort which also hosts a museum dedicated to the medieval and Renaissance periods. Afterwards take some time to poke around the abandoned cliffside neighbourhood of Via delle Rovine.

End your day in the most dramatic of the Maremma's hill towns, **Pitigliano** (see p127). Make sure you arrive by 5pm in order to enter the town's ultramodern archaeological museum, set within a fortified palazzo. The town's labyrinthine Jewish ghetto and museum is open a little later. Then head to the panoramic balcony just beyond the eastern gate to watch the evening lights come on over a town that seems to grow from bare rock.

See map on pp126–7 ←

Leisure Activities

Parco Naturale della Maremma

1 Parco Naturale della Maremma and Monti dell'Uccellina Trails

MAP E6 ▪ 0564 393 238 ▪ Some trails occasionally closed Jun–Sep ▪ Adm ▪ www.parco-maremma.it

"Strada degli Olivi" goes to the beach. Trail 1 (7.2 km/4.5 miles) explores San Rabano abbey's ruins. Trail 2 (6 km/4 miles) goes past medieval towers to the rocky shore. Trail 3 (9.6 km/6 miles) explores prehistoric caves. Trail 4 (12 km/7.5 miles) wanders everywhere.

2 Exploring Etruscan Tombs

MAP F6 ▪ www.leviecave.it

Get a map in Sovana or at Sorano's fortress to explore the tombs and *vie cave* hidden in the countryside.

3 Saturnia's Hot Springs

MAP E6

Be sure to relax in the mineral-rich hot springs here *(see p66)*.

4 Elba's Beaches

MAP C5

Visit beaches tucked away on the northeast shore. The western coast is good for snorkelling and Fetovaia has sandy beaches on tiny inlets.

5 Scuba and Snorkelling on Elba

MAP C5 ▪ Elba Diving Centre, Viale Aldo Moro 42, Marciana Marina ▪ 3397 338 902 ▪ www.elbadiving.it

Basic lessons, full courses, rentals and guided day and night dives.

6 Sailing and Windsurfing on Elba

MAP C5 ▪ Aloha Center, Lido di Capoliveri ▪ 3474 969 219 ▪ www.alohacenter.it

Rent sailboards, catamarans and Zodiacs, or take windsurfing and sailing courses.

7 Horse Riding on the Coast

MAP E6 ▪ Maneggio Il Barbazzale, Via Aurelia Nord Km 146, Orbetello Scalo ▪ 0564 864 208, 3200 813 831 ▪ www.maneggioilbarbazzale.com

Guided rides set off from an Orbetello lagoon base. Moonlit rides take place from June to September.

8 Hiking on Elba

MAP C5

Tourist office brochures lay out 12 hikes from 90 minutes to all day. The most rewarding is up (or down – you may ride the cable car one way) the Monte Capenne, past Santuario di San Cerbone church.

9 Scuba around Monte Argentario

MAP E6 ▪ Pelagos Diving Centre, Lungomare A Doria 12–14, Porto Ercole ▪ 0564 834 200 ▪ www.pelagosdc.com

Equipment rentals, lessons, guided dives and snorkelling around the islands of Giglio and Giannutri and Monte Argentario.

10 Etruscan Coast Beaches

MAP C3

The "Etruscan Coast" to the south of Livorno includes pine-shaded, sandy, semi-secluded Marina di Albarese and the resort of San Vincenzo.

Restaurants

PRICE CATEGORIES
For a three-course meal for one with half
a bottle of wine (or equivalent meal),
taxes and extra charges.

€ under €35   €€ €35–70   €€€ over €70

1 Ristorante Gli Attortellati, Grosseto

MAP E5 ▪ Strada Provinciale 40
Trappola 39 ▪ 0564 400 059
▪ Open Tue–Fri D, Sat, Sun L
▪ Closed Mon ▪ €€

Advance booking is essential at this
award-winning *agriturismo* serving
delicious Maremmana dishes.

2 Da Caino, Montemerano

MAP E6 ▪ Via Canonica, 3
▪ 0564 602 817 ▪ €€€

A rustic but elegant room in the
Maremma. The cooking is inspired
by local recipes and seasonal
ingredients. Bread and pasta are
homemade, and the wine list is vast.

3 Il Tufo Allegro, Pitigliano

MAP F6 ▪ Vicolo della Constituzione
5 ▪ 0564 616 192 ▪ Closed Tue, Wed L
(except Aug) ▪ €€€

A young-spirited place, where
Domenico adds creative touches to
local ingredients and Valeria suggests
accompanying wines.

4 Osteria del Noce, Elba

MAP C5 ▪ Via della Madonna
14, Marciana ▪ 0565 901 284 ▪ €€

The softly lit rustic dining room has
a pergola-shaded terrace with sea
views. The owners' Ligurian roots
are evident in the cooking.

5 Ristorante nel Buco, Castiglione della Pescaia

MAP D5 ▪ Via della Libertà 93
▪ 3392 878 439 ▪ €

Small cellar *osteria* in this fishing
village/resort. The food is excellent,
balancing meat and seafood, and
the owner carries a good tune.

6 Osteria Ferraja, Elba

MAP C5 ▪ Calata Matteotti 12,
Portoferraio ▪ 0565 190 1473 ▪ €€

Dine portside in a scenic spot. Grilled
fish or a *fritto misto* (catch-dependent
mixed fry) are good choices, but also
try traditional dishes like *riso nero*
(rice blackened with squid ink).

7 La Barcaccina, San Vincenzo

MAP C4 ▪ Via del Faro ▪ 3939 699 237
▪ Closed Nov–Mar & Wed ▪ €€

Kick off your shoes for some serious
seafood cooking right on the sand.

8 Publius, Elba

MAP C5 ▪ Piazza Castagneto
11, Poggio, Marciana ▪ 0565 99 208
▪ Closed Nov–Mar ▪ €€

Family-run for four decades, this
refined restaurant has a jaw-
dropping perch in the Elban hills.

9 La Taverna Etrusca, Sovana

MAP F6 ▪ Piazza del Pretorio 16
▪ 0564 614 113 ▪ €

Good Tuscan cuisine in a room
framed by beamed ceilings and
stone archways dating to the 1200s.

10 Emanuel, Elba

MAP C5 ▪ Loc Enfola, near
Portoferraio ▪ 3802 462 220 ▪ Closed
25 Dec–Apr & Mon ▪ €€€

An unassuming beachfront shack
serving Elba's best seafood and
excellent desserts. The tiny courtyard at the back leads onto the
pebble beach.

The pleasant courtyard at Emanuel

See map on pp126–7 ←

Streetsmart

A pair of Vespa scooters on a street
in Arezzo, Eastern Tuscany

Getting Around

Arriving by Air

Almost all transatlantic and intercontinental flights to Italy land in **Rome Fiumicino** or **Milan Malpensa**, from where you can get connecting flights to Pisa or to Florence. Rome and Milan both also have very fast train links to Florence. Alternatively, you can rent a car and drive to Tuscany from Rome or Milan.

Pisa Galileo Galilei, the biggest international airport in Tuscany, has many connections to the UK and to most other European countries. The PisaMover transit service (operated by Trenitalia) takes only 5 or 6 minutes from the airport to Pisa Centrale station, which is then about an hour by train to Florence, half an hour to Lucca or 2 hours to Siena.

Florence Peretola (Amerigo Vespucci) airport is smaller and offers direct flights to major European capitals and business cities. It is situated about 4 km (2 miles) from the city centre. Taxis wait outside the front of the terminal and charge a fixed price to central Florence. Located near the airport terminals, the **T2 Vespucci tram** provides a convenient and fast connection to Florence. Trams run frequently (every five minutes at peak times), seven days a week, and take just 20 minutes from the airport to the central train station.

International Train Travel

Regular trains connect Italy to the main towns and cities in France, Switzerland, Austria and Eastern Europe, and journeys should be reserved in advance. You can buy tickets and passes for multiple international journeys via **Eurail** or **Interrail**; however, you may still need to pay an additional reservation fee depending on which rail service you travel with. Always check that your pass is valid before boarding.

Regional Trains

Trenitalia is the main operator in Italy; safety and hygiene measures and ticket information can be found online. Tickets for journeys on standard trains *(Regionale)* in Tuscany can also be bought at tobacconists and lottery outlets.

High-speed rail services (*alta velocità* or AV) are provided from Florence and Pisa to cities outside the region by Trenitalia. Private company **Italo Treno** also offers high-speed services, but these go only from Florence. High-speed trains need reservations with allocated seating. For the cheapest prices, book between 90 and 120 days in advance. Note that of Florence's ten railway stations, Santa Maria Novella is its central hub. Train tickets must be validated before boarding

by stamping them in machines at the entrance to platforms. Fines are applied if you are found with an unvalidated ticket; if for any reason you are unable to validate a ticket before boarding go immediately to the ticket inspector.

Public Transport

Most Tuscan towns and cities provide efficient local bus services (plus trams in Florence), but the more rural areas are often poorly served and can be slightly unreliable, especially on Sundays and public holidays when a reduced timetable is in operation.

Buses and Trams

Tickets should be bought in advance and are available from dedicated kiosks, newsagents and tobacconists as well as some bars; ten-journey tickets can be bought at a reduced rate (€14/ €11). All tickets must be validated at the time of boarding; validation machines can be found inside the bus or tram. Tickets are also available on board from the driver but cost more (€2.50). Ticket prices are standardized in Tuscany, with one rate for the ten provincial capitals (€1.50) and another for elsewhere (€1.20); local transport tickets for one town are not valid in another.

Florence's two tram lines, T1 and T2, run from 5am to midnight (extended to 1:30 or 2am on Friday and Saturday) through the centre of the city from the suburb of Scandicci to the main hospital, Careggi.

Long-Distance Bus Travel

Long-distance buses are the best way to reach many destinations within Tuscany, particularly the hilly or mountainous areas of the region which not served by railways or where stations are at a distance from the historic centre. **Autolinee Toscane** connects Mugello and north-eastern Tuscany with Florence and Arezzo, north and much of the west (including the island of Elba). **Tiemme** operates throughout the southern half of the region. Long-distance services within Italy, including numerous Tuscan destinations, are provided by **Autolinee Baltour**. **Flixbus** runs a low-cost bus service to many other Italian cities and a range of European destinations.

Guided Bus Tours

City Sightseeing is one of the area's best tour bus companies. It runs hop-on hop-off tours around Florence and Livorno with audioguides in a variety of languages.

Taxis

Taxis in Italy aren't particularly cheap. Official registered taxis in the country are white and can be found in strategic locations around all Tuscan cities; note that it is illegal for taxis to stop in the street if hailed. Unofficial taxis should be avoided, as should drivers who come into stations or airports offering their services; official taxi drivers do not do this. Tariffs are displayed inside taxis and a meter should be visible and running during the entire journey, except for fixed-tariff journeys, such as from Florence Peretola airpot or Pisa Galileo Galilei to the city centre. Additional charges may be added for large loads of luggage and journeys at night. If you are planning a long journey by taxi it's a good idea to ask for an estimate cost before leaving. There is a long list of estimated fees for out-of-town destinations from Pisa on the **Cotapi** official taxi website. Many taxis do not accept credit card payments so if you wish to pay by card, specify this when calling or ask if the service is available before leaving. Those in groups of more than three people or those with specific requirements or trans-porting a considerable amount of luggage should specify this information when booking, to ensure that a suitable vehicle is sent. Taxis can be ordered online or by phone from **4242** or **4390** in Florence and **RadioTaxi Pisa** in Pisa.

DIRECTORY

ARRIVING BY AIR

Florence Peretola
W aeroporto.firenze.it

Milan Malpensa
W milanomalpensa-airport.com/en/

Pisa Galileo Galilei
W pisa-airport.com

Rome Fiumicino
W adr.it

T2 Vespucci tram
W gestramvia.it

INTERNATIONAL TRAIN TRAVEL

Eurorail
W eurorail.com

Interrail
W interrail.eu

REGIONAL TRAINS

Italo Treno
W italotreno.it

Trenitalia
W trenitalia.com

LONG-DISTANCE BUS TRAVEL

Autolinee Baltour
W baltour.it

Autolinee Toscane
W autolineetoscane.it

CTT Nord
W cttnord.it

Flixbus
W flixbus.it

Tiemme
W tiemmespa.it

GUIDED BUS TOURS

City Sightseeing
W city-sightseeing.it

TAXI

4242
W 4242.it

4390
W 4390.it

Cotapi, Pisa
W cotapi.it

RadioTaxi Pisa
W cotapi.it/en

Driving

A road trip through Tuscany is the best way to see the more remote parts of the region and gives you the freedom to choose when and where to go. However, it can also be a hair-raising experience at times. Italians have a reputation for driving erratically, so make sure you are familiar with the rules of the road before you embark.

Driving to Florence and Tuscany

Florence and Tuscany are easily reached from other European countries via the International European Road Network that connects major roads across national borders within Europe. Once in Italy, the A1 motorway (autostrada) runs from north to south from Milan to Naples, passing through Florence and Tuscany, while the A12, intended to link Genoa to Rome along Italy's west coast, currently ends just south of Livorno before reappearing in Lazio for the last section to Rome. The A11 links Florence to Pisa via Prato, Pistoia and Lucca. Tolls are payable on motorways in Tuscany and in most of Italy; drivers must take a ticket from an automatic machine on entering the motorway and this is used to calculate the toll automatically at the exit. To avoid queuing to leave the motorway, pay by credit card and choose one of the lanes designated for card payments or invest in a prepaid Viacard, available at one of the Punto Blu offices near many motorway exits. Avoid the dedicated Telepass lanes, which are for Telepass account holders with the relevant electronic reader. If you wish to avoid toll roads, there is usually an alternative route signposted. In Italy road signs for motorways are green, whereas toll-free main roads have blue signs. The **ACI** (Automobile Club d'Italia) website has a section in English with useful information for visiting motorists.

Car Rental

To rent a car in Italy you must be over 18 and have a valid EU driving licence or International Driving Permit. Most rental companies require you to have held a licence for at least one year, some have a minimum age of 21 and most apply young driver surcharges for under 25s. You also need to have a credit card as guarantee. Local outfits are rarely cheaper than the web, so it is wise to prebook from home. Try well-known rental sites such as **Auto Europe**.

Driving in Florence and Tuscany

Many of the region's cities, towns and villages have well-preserved historic centres that are only accessible to residents' vehicles; other cars entering the limited traffic zone (*zona a traffico limitato*, or ZTL) are subject to fines. Florence has several vehicle-sharing companies, including **TiMove, Enjoy** and **BIT Mobility**. All three are allowed to enter and park in the ZTL zone – these are a good option for those who only need transportation for a few hours. If you're staying at a hotel in the centre, ask in advance about access; this is usually possible, at least for depositing and collecting bags, but you will need to advise staff of your registration number to avoid incurring fines. It's a good idea to park outside the centre and explore on foot, even where there isn't a limited traffic zone, as the narrow and steep streets of many areas can be challenging. Parking spaces marked with blue lines are subject to payment and there should be a meter nearby; yellow lines signal restrictions such as parking for residents or the disabled only, or for loading and unloading, while white lines indicate free parking.

Many filling stations close on Sundays, though often there are automated dispensers that accept banknotes and sometimes credit cards.

Rules of the Road

Drive on the right, use the left lane only for passing, and give way to traffic from the right. Seat belts are required for all passengers in the front and back, and heavy fines are levied for using a mobile phone while driving. During the day dipped headlights are compulsory when driving on motorways, dual carriageways and on all out-of-town roads. A red warning triangle and fluorescent vest must be carried at all times, for use in the event of an emergency. Between mid-November and mid-April it is obligatory to carry winter tyres or snow-chains on all vehicles except motorcycles. If you have an accident or break-down, switch on your hazard warning lights and place a warning triangle 50 m (55 yd) behind your vehicle. In the event of a breakdown, call the **ACI** freephone emergency line (803-116 from an Italian phone; 800-116800 from a non-Italian mobile phone) or the emergency services. (112 or 113). The legal drink-drive limit is strictly enforced. If you are drinking any alcohol, use public transport or take a taxi.

Hitchhiking

Hitchhiking (autostop) is illegal on motorways, and is not commonplace in large cities such as Florence. In more rural areas it is an uncommon but not unheard of transport method for travellers on a budget. Always consider your own safety before entering an unknown vehicle.

Cycle and Scooter Hire

Tuscany has more *strade bianche* – gravel surfaced "white roads" – than any other Italian region, and they are great for explor-ing the countryside by bike. Tour company **yubike** offers unique bike trips around the region. **I Bike Italy** also runs

several itineraries, including Florence day tours and multiday trips around the region of Chianti. **Florence by Bike** and numerous other agencies also rent out city bikes, race bikes, mountain bikes and e-bikes, and most hotels can organize this, some-times with special rates. Bike-sharing schemes also operate in most of Tuscany's major cities. The **Piste Ciclabili** website has an interactive map of cycle paths in Italy.

Scooters are another great way to see more of the countryside and they can be hired from many places around the region, especially in the Chianti area and in the city of Florence. An ordinary driving licence is suffi-cient for vehicles up to 125cc in Italy; helmets must be worn at all times whilst riding the scooter.

Walking

Wandering around Tuscany's main cities and towns is one of the most enjoyable aspects of any trip to this picturesque area. Many urban areas are largely pedestrianized and it's often easier to travel by foot than by bus. No historic town centre in Tuscany takes more than 30 minutes to cross on foot. You can stop at viewpoints, pop into local cafés and easily take in several of the main tourist sights within a couple of hours. Many streets are cobblestoned, however, so wear com-fortable shoes. There are also many scenic long walks and hikes through Tuscany's countryside.

Ferries

Toremar is the main ferry company for travellers going to Elba and the islands of the archipelago. It operates from the ports of Livorno (to Gorgona and Capraia), Piombino (to Portoferraio, Cavo and Rio Marina on Elba and to Pianosa) and Porto Santo Stefano (to Capraia and Giannutri). Hydrofoil ser-vices are also available for Cavo and Portoferraio on Elba. Advance booking is advisable. Get to the port at least an hour early if taking a car.

DIRECTORY

DRIVING TO FLORENCE AND TUSCANY

ACI
w aci.it

CAR RENTAL

Auto Europe
w autoeurope.com

DRIVING IN FLORENCE AND TUSCANY

BIT Mobility
w bitmobility.it

Enjoy
w enjoy.enl.com

TiMove
w timove.com

CYCLE AND SCOOTER HIRE

Florence by Bike
w florencebybike.it

I Bike Italy
w ibikeitaly.com

Piste Ciclabili
w piste-ciclabili.com

yubike
w yubiketours.com

FERRIES

Toremar
w toremar.it

Practical Information

Passports and Visas

For entry requirements, including visas, consult your nearest Italian embassy or check the **Ministero degli Affari Esteri** website. From late 2023, citizens of the UK, US, Canada, Australia and New Zealand do not need a visa for stays of up to three months, but must apply in advance for the European Travel Information and Authorization System (**ETIAS**). Visitors from other countries may also require an ETIAS, so check before travelling. EU nationals do not need a visa or an ETIAS.

Government Advice

Now more than ever, it is important to consult both your and the Italian government's advice before travelling. The **UK Foreign, Commonwealth & Development Office (FCDO)**, the **US State Department** and the **Australian Department of Foreign Affairs and Trade** and the Italian **Ministero della Salute** offer the latest information on security, health and local regulations.

Customs Information

You can find information on the laws relating to goods and currency taken in or out of Italy on the **ENIT** (Italy's national tourist board) website. For EU citizens no limits or duties are applied on most goods carried in or out of Italy as long as they are for personal use only. Exceptions include firearms and weapons, certain types of food and plants, endangered species, pets, drugs and over €10,000 in cash.

Prescription medicines should be in original containers, and you should carry the prescription. Travellers cannot bring in meat or milk from outside Europe, and must declare any animal products, fruit, vegetables or plants on arrival. Non-EU residents can also claim back sales tax on purchases over €155.

Insurance

We recommend that you take out a comprehensive insurance policy covering theft, loss of belongings, medical care, cancellations and delays, and read the small print carefully.

UK citizens are eligible for free emergency medical care in Italy provided they have a valid European Health Insurance Card (EHIC) or UK Global Health Insurance Card (**GHIC**).

Health

Italy has a world-class healthcare system. Emergency medical care in Italy is free for all EU and Australian citizens. If you have an EHIC or GHIC, or Australian Medicare card, be sure to present this as soon as possible. You may have to pay for treatment and reclaim the money later.

For visitors coming from outside the EU and Australia, payment of hospital and other medical expenses is the patient's responsibility. It is therefore important to arrange comprehensive medical insurance before travelling.

The most central hospital in Florence is **Ospedale Santa Maria Nuova**. Italian pharmacies *(farmacie)* are signalled by a green cross and are usually well equipped in treating minor ailments. The central **Farmacia Comunale di Santa Maria Novella** in Florence is open 24/7.

Italian water is safe to drink except from train taps and any source indicated *"acqua non potabile"*. No vaccinations are required to visit Italy.

Smoking, Alcohol and Drugs

Smoking is banned in enclosed public places. Possession of narcotics is prohibited and could result in a prison sentence. Italy has a strict limit of 0.5g/l BAC (blood alcohol content) for drivers. This means that you cannot drink more than one small beer or a small glass of wine if you plan to drive. For drivers with less than three years' driving experience the limit is 0.

ID

By law you must carry identification with you at all times in Italy. A photocopy of your passport photo page (and visa if applicable) should suffice. If you are stopped by the police you may be asked to present the original document within 12 hours.

Personal Security

While Italy is generally safe and violent crime is rare, it is best to exercise caution. All travellers should avoid deserted back streets and empty parks at night. Pickpockets operate on buses, around stations and in other busy spots. Any lost property found on a bus or train in Florence is sent to the **Ufficio Oggetti Smarriti**.

The ambulance, police and fire brigade can be reached on the Europe-wide **emergency (Carabinieri)** number 112. The operators speak English.There are also dedicated lines for the **ambulance** and the **fire brigade**.

There are two police forces, the Carabinieri,

the military branch, and the **Polizia di Stato**, the civil branch. The **Questura di Firenze** (*polizia* headquarters) is centrally located. You must report crimes if you wish to make an insurance claim.

Many Italians drive aggressively, so be careful behind the wheel.

As a rule, Italians are very accepting of all people, regardless of their race, gender or sexuality. Homosexuality was legalized in 1887 and in 1982, Italy became the third country to recognise the right to legally change your gender. If you do feel unsafe in Florence, the **Safe Space Alliance** pinpoints your nearest place of refuge.

Women may sometimes receive unwanted and unwelcome male attention, especially around tourist areas. If you feel threatened, head straight for the nearest police station.

Travellers with Specific Requirements

Many of Tuscany's town centres have steep and cobbled streets, presenting difficulties for visitors with reduced mobility. Travellers with reduced mobility are admitted free to most sights, and many places have adaptations for visually impaired visitors, including the Uffizi's tactile tours.

Hotels generally have at least one accessible room on offer. However, many historic properties are unable to provide suitable accommodation for guests with limited mobility.

RFI (Rete Ferroviaria Italiana) provides help at railway stations; details are online and at the Sala Blu point at Florence's Santa Maria Novella station. To book an adapted taxi, call 4242 or 4390 *(see p135)* 24 hours ahead. **Moveris** also services travellers with specific requirements.

DIRECTORY

PASSPORTS AND VISAS
ETIAS
🅦 etiasvisa.com
Ministero degli Affari Esteri
🅦 vistoperitalia.esteri.it

GOVERNMENT ADVICE
Australian Department of Foreign Affairs and Trade
🅦 smartraveller.gov.au
Ministero della Salute
🅦 salute.gov.it
UK Foreign, Commonwealth & Development Office (FCDO)
🅦 gov.uk/foreign-travel-advice
US State Department
🅦 travel.state.gov

CUSTOMS INFORMATION
ENIT
🅦 italia.it

INSURANCE
GHIC
🅦 ghic.org.uk

HEALTH
Farmacia Comunale di Santa Maria Novella
MAP L1 ■ Piazza della Stazione 1
🅒 055 216 761
Ospedale Santa Maria Nuova
MAP P3 ■ Piazza Santa Maria Nuova 1
🅦 uslcentro.toscana.it

PERSONAL SECURITY
Ambulance
🅒 118

Emergency (Carabinieri)
🅒 112
Fire Brigade
🅒 115
Polizia di Stato
🅒 113
🅦 poliziadistato.it
Questura di Firenze
Via Zara 2
🅒 055 49 771
Ufficio Oggetti Smarriti
Via Veracini 5
🅒 055 334 802
Safe Space Alliance
🅦 safespacealliance.com

TRAVELLERS WITH SPECIFIC REQUIREMENTS
Moveris
🅦 moveris.it
RFI
🅦 rfi.it

Time Zone

Italy operates on Central European Time (CET), which is one hour ahead of Greenwich Mean Time and six hours ahead of US Eastern Standard Time. The clock moves forward one hour during daylight saving time from the last Sunday in March until the last Sunday in October.

Money

Italy is one of the 19 European countries using the euro (€). Most establishments accept major credit, debit and prepaid currency cards. Contactless payments are more common in Florence, but it's always a good idea to carry some cash for transport tickets, as well as for smaller items. Cash is also necessary when visiting markets or more rural areas of Tuscany. Tipping is not expected in restaurants or by taxi drivers, but hotel porters and housekeeping will expect €1 per bag or day.

Electrical Appliances

Italian electricity runs on 220V/50Hz. To use a 110V device, you will need a converter, however most new appliances are dual voltage. To plug in, you will need an adaptor that fits continental Europe's standard two round pins.

Mobile Phones and Wi-Fi

Almost every hotel now provides Wi-Fi, usually free, and there are free Wi-Fi hotspots in squares and public buildings in many cities. Florence's **Firenze Card** includes three days of Wi-Fi and the Mercato Centrale has free Wi-Fi upstairs. In smaller towns, you may find internet in a store or bar. The **WiFi Italia** app allows you to connect quickly and easily to free Wi-Fi hotspots.

Visitors with EU tariffs will be able to use their devices abroad without being affected by roaming charges. This means that you pay the same rates as you would at home.

Non-EU members can purchase an Italian SIM card (you will need ID).

Postal Services

Italy's post service, **Poste Italiane**, while improving, can be slow. Florence's **Central Post Office** is a 4-minute walk south of the Duomo. However, you needn't visit a post office (*ufficio postale*) to send a letter; tobacconists or newsagents can sell the right stamps (*francobolli*). Drop your letters in the postbox slot (usually red) that is labelled *"per tutte le altre destinazioni"*, not *"per la città"*.

Weather

Tuscany has a generally warm climate, although the July and August heat can be brutal, especially in landlocked Florence. It snows in the hills in midwinter, and cold winds come from the Apennine mountains. Spring's middle ground keeps hotels booked, but autumn, when grapes (September) and olives (October) are harvested and boar and truffles hunted, is the true Tuscan time of year.

It is wise to bring one nice outfit, although few restaurants require jacket and tie. Many churches do not allow you to enter with bare shoulders or knees; a scarf or light shawl draped around the waist or shoulders is essential. You must also wear shoes when entering churches and cathedrals.

Opening Hours

Shops, businesses and churches traditionally open at 8 or 9am, shut for *pausa pranzo* (lunch break) from 12:30 or 1pm to 3pm, then reopen until 6 to 8pm. In larger cities, however, the *pranzo* is disappearing in favour of *orario continuato* (straight through) for chain stores and other shops. Post office hours are usually 8:20am–7pm weekdays, 8:20am–12:30pm on Saturdays. Standard banking hours are usually 8:30am to 1 or 1:30pm and from 3 until 4:15pm, weekends. Museum opening times vary, but 9am to 5pm is common. A few still close during the *pranzo*, especially outside big cities.

Italian national holidays are: New Year's Day, Epiphany (6 Jan), Easter Sunday and Monday, Liberation Day (25 Apr), Workers' Day (1 May), Republic Day (2 Jun), *Ferragosto* (15 Aug), All Saints' Day (1 Nov), Immaculate Conception (8 Dec), Christmas Day (25 Dec) and St Stephen's Day (26 Dec). Several services, particularly those aimed at locals, close on these days. Towns also shut down for the feast day of their saint (17 Jun in Pisa; 24 Jun in Florence).

The COVID-19 pandemic proved that situations can change suddenly. Always check before visiting attractions and hospitality venues for up-to-date hours and booking requirements.

Visitor Information

The state tourism board ENIT (p138) provides basic information. Official tourist offices are better for detailed information and inspiration. **Florence Tourism** has five offices in the city (including at the airport and main train station), all listed on their website. The **Tuscany Regional Tourism** and **Visit Tuscany** websites portal are also useful.

In Florence, the Firenze Card provides entry to many museums and sites and is valid for 72 hours from its first use. The Firenzecard+ also covers public transport and can be used for discounts at affiliated restaurants and shops. Local *informazioni turistiche* offices (often signed "Pro Loco") are good for free maps, opening hours and hotel directories, and usually respond to email requests for specific assistance.

Local Customs

You can be fined for dropping litter and sitting on steps outside certain monuments and it is an offence to climb into public fountains. Illegal street traders operate in many of Tuscany's city centres; avoid making any purchases from them as you could be fined by the local police. It is also illegal to take sand and shells from Tuscany's beaches (except during specially authorized trips, such as the mineral-hunting experiences organized on Elba).

Taxes and Refunds

VAT (value-added tax) is usually 22%. Under certain conditions, non-EU citizens can claim a refund. Claim the rebate before you buy (show your passport to the shop assistant and complete a form) and later present a Customs officer with your receipts as you leave. Bring stamped receipts back to the vendor to issue a refund. Information is available from international taxfree shopping organizations such as **Global Blue**.

Accommodation

Florence and Tuscany offer a huge variety of accommodation – from working farms to monastery stays. Hotels are categorized from 1 (basic) to 5 (deluxe) stars, based on amenities rather than charm or location. At 3 stars and above, all rooms have at least a private bathroom. During peak season lodgings fill up and prices become inflated, so book in advance. All accommodation providers are obliged to add a tourist tax to rates. This varies from €1 to €5 per night, for a maximum of 7 nights; under 12s are exempt. Always check if the tourist tax is included in quoted rates. Under Italian law, hotels are required to register guests at police headquarters and issue a receipt of payment.

Budget travellers should look for accommodation in tourist offices. Most keep a list of *affittacamere* (cheap room rentals), which can range from semi-private access and a lovely room to a cramped spare room in someone's apartment.

An extra bed costs around 30 per cent more, but it is sometimes free for under-14s in the parents' room).

DIRECTORY

MOBILE PHONES AND WI-FI
Firenze Card
w firenzecard.it
WiFi Italia
w wifi.italia.it

POSTAL SERVICES
Central Post Office
MAP M4 ◼ Via Pellicceria 3
☎ 055 273 6481
Poste Italiane
w poste.it

VISITOR INFORMATION
Florence Tourism
MAP N2 ◼ Via Cavour 1/R
◼ Open 9am–1pm Mon–Fri
w feelflorence.it
Tuscany Regional Tourism
w visittuscany.com/en

TAXES AND REFUNDS
Global Blue
w globalblue.com

Places to Stay

Luxury Hotels

Castel Monastero, outside Siena
MAP E4 ▪ Monastero d'Ombrone 19, Castelnuovo Berardenga ▪ www.castelmonastero.com ▪ €€€
With vaulted ceilings and exposed stone walls, this 11th-century castle turned luxury retreat offers views over the pretty vine-covered countryside. It also has two incredible restaurants (where Gordon Ramsey serves as chef consultant), a spa and wellness centre, and two swimming pools on site.

Belmond Villa San Michele, Fiesole
MAP E2 ▪ Via Doccia 4 ▪ 0555 678 200 ▪ Wi-Fi ▪ www.belmond.com/villa-san-michele-florence ▪ €€€
Michelangelo is said to have designed the façade of this 15th-century former Franciscan monastery that stands between Florence and Fiesole. The original building has only double rooms, with the sumptuous suites hiding in half-buried wings overlooking the terraced gardens and heated pool. The large wooded park has a walking trail, and there is also a gym.

Castiglion del Bosco, near Montalcino
MAP E4 ▪ Loc Castiglion del Bosco ▪ 0577 191 3750 ▪ Wi-Fi ▪ www.castigliondelbosco.com ▪ €€€
Situated in the beautiful Val d'Orcia (a UNESCO World Heritage Site) in the Brunello di Montalcino wine region, this resort stands next to the pilgrim route of Via Francigena. The 800-year-old rural estate has been transformed into a chic hideaway with a heated infinity pool, a spa, a golf course and a winery. Rooms and suites are in the old Borgo, and 17th- and 18th-century stone farmhouses are now luxury villas with private, heated pools. The views are sublime.

Four Seasons, Florence
MAP Q1 ▪ Borgo Pinti 99 ▪ 0552 6261 ▪ Wi-Fi ▪ www.fourseasons.com/florence ▪ €€€
A genuine Renaissance palace surrounded by one of the largest private gardens in Florence and featuring a spa and an outdoor pool, the Four Seasons is the ultimate city retreat. The rooms and suites range from the large and luxurious to the downright palatial, some retaining original frescoes and expertly restored stucco work. The service is five-star.

Gallia Palace, Punta Ala
MAP D5 ▪ Via delle Sughere, Punta Ala ▪ 0564 922 022 ▪ Wi-Fi ▪ www.galliapalace.it ▪ €€€
The top hotel in Tuscany's most exclusive coastal resort, the Gallia Palace has large, tasteful rooms, a beauty spa, a swimming pool in the park, a private beach with boats and canoes and access to a neighbouring golf course. Weekend candlelit dinners take place on the lawn.

Helvetia e Bristol, Florence
MAP M3 ▪ Via de Pescioni 2 ▪ 0552 6651 ▪ Wi-Fi ▪ www.collezione.starhotels.com ▪ €€€
Although lacking all the amenities at the Excelsior and Villa San Michele's setting, the Helvetia still feels posher than either. The most central of the city's luxury hotels, this has been operating since the 19th century and has welcomed distinguished guests, including composer Igor Stravinsky and writer Bertrand Russell.

Il Pellicano, Monte Argentario
MAP E6 ▪ Loc Sbarcatello ▪ 0564 858 111 ▪ Wi-Fi ▪ www.hotelilpellicano.com/it ▪ €€€
An oasis of luxury on a wild and scenic bit of the Maremma coast, the original house was built by American socialites Patricia and Michael Graham for themselves and their friends. Now an exclusive hotel with a delightful hint of retro atmosphere, Il Pellicano

consists of a villa and cottages among cypress, pine and olive woods. Amenities include a piano bar, gym, tennis courts, a heated seawater pool, spa and water-skiing facilities.

Villa Ottone, Elba

MAP C5 ■ Loc Ottone ■ 0565 933 042 ■ www. villaottone.com ■ €€

This is the classiest place to stay on Elba, especially if you have a room in the original 19th-century villa. But even the 1970s main building has terraces with sea views. There's also a spa offering Turkish baths, Ayurveda treatments and Thai massage, plus a pool, tennis court and watersports equipment.

Villa Scacciapensieri, outside Siena

MAP E4 ■ Strada di Scacciapensieri 10 ■ 057 741 441 ■ www.villa scacciapensieri.it ■ €€€

Set in a 19th-century villa just outside Siena over-looking the city walls in hilly parkland, the villa has spacious rooms, including three suites. Meals are served on the terraces, and there are tennis courts and a pool. Enjoy both Siena (whose historic core is only a few kilometres away) and savour the beautiful countryside and views of the hills of Chianti.

Westin Excelsior, Florence

MAP K3 ■ Piazza Ognissanti 3 ■ 0552 7151 ■ Wi-Fi ■ www.westin florence.com ■ €€€

The top address in town, this is a bastion of luxury and refinement set in a Renaissance palace on the Arno. There are few

amenities that the hotel lacks or services it cannot provide. In-room spa treatments are available, and you can book a room equipped with a treadmill or stationary bike. Try to get an Arno-side room. The penthouse rooms have stunning views of the Duomo and the river.

Historic Hotels

Hotel della Fortezza, Sorano

MAP F5–6 ■ Piazza Cairoli 9 ■ 0564 633 549 ■ Closed Jan & Feb ■ www.hoteldella fortezza.com ■ €€

This lovely hotel is installed in a wing of Sorano's 11th-century Fortezza degli Orsini *(see p129)*. The comfortable rooms come with wooden ceilings, 19th-century furnishings and fantastic countryside views. With the high breezes flowing through here, there is no need for air conditioning.

L'Antico Pozzo, San Gimignano

MAP D3 ■ Via San Matteo 87 ■ 0577 942 014 ■ Wi-Fi ■ www. anticopozzo.com ■ €€

Although predominantly 15th century, bits of the building date back to the Middle Ages. Its name comes from an ancient well on the site that was used, the story goes, to hang young women who resisted the medieval *droit de seigneur* law. In the 17th century it hosted Inquisition trials. Large rooms and iron bedsteads lend an antique air, while the "superior" rooms come with the original 17th-century frescoes.

Morandi alla Crocetta, Florence

MAP P2 ■ Via Laura 50 ■ 0552 344 747 ■ Wi-Fi ■ www.hotel morandi.it ■ €€

Built as a convent in 1511, the charming Morandi is located in the historic centre of the city. Some of the beams, antiques and artwork are reproductions, but the frescoes are genuine 16th century.

Palazzo Ravizza, Siena

MAP E4 ■ Pian de Mantellini 34 ■ 0577 280 462 ■ Wi-Fi ■ www. palazzoravizza.it ■ €€

Some rooms at this family-run 17th-century hotel retain their frescoes and those at the back are quiet and offer garden views.

Royal Victoria, Pisa

MAP C3 ■ Lungarno Pacinotti 12 ■ 050 940 111 ■ Wi-Fi ■ www.royal victoria.it ■ €€

Opened in 1839, this is Pisa's oldest hotel and has had John Ruskin and Theodore Roosevelt as guests. It is not as grand as it once was, but still oozes history and has a prime location on the Arno. Some doubles link to make family suites, and there's a private parking garage for guests.

Villa di STR, Siena

MAP E4 ■ Viale Vittorio Veneto 11 ■ 0577 188 2807 ■ www.lavilladi str.it ■ €€

In an Art Nouveau-style villa located just outside the city walls, this boutique hotel has a lovely garden and many rooms have pri-vate balconies. It is known for its hearty breakfasts.

Villa Pitiana, Florence

MAP E3 ▪ Via Provinciale per Tosi 7 ▪ 055 860 259 ▪ Wi-Fi ▪ www.villa pitiana.com ▪ €€

This much-altered former monastery is set in a park on the outskirts of Florence and has hosted Galileo and Petrarch. The villa has a decent restaurant and an outdoor pool.

Albergo Pietrasanta, Pietrasanta

MAP C2 ▪ Via Garibaldi 35 ▪ 0584 793 726 ▪ www. albergopietrasanta.com ▪ €€

This 17th-century palazzo is an exclusive hotel, with baths sheathed in the marbles of this mining town between Forte dei Marmi and Viareggio.

Castello Banfi, Montalcino

MAP E4 ▪ Castello di Poggio alle Mura ▪ 0577 877 700 ▪ www.banfi.it/ en ▪ €€€

This small resort on the Banfi Estate (see p70) occupies a castle dating from the 12th century. The annexed buildings are part of the original medieval village and one-of-a-kind rooms offer views of the surrounding vineyards.

Loggiato dei Serviti, Florence

MAP P2 ▪ Piazza Santissima Annunziata 3 ▪ 055 289 592 ▪ www.loggiatodei servitihotel.it ▪ €€

High Renaissance-styled rooms in a 1527 building designed by Antonio da Sangallo the Elder. The best, if slightly noisier, rooms open onto a magnificent loggia overlooking the square. Canopy beds add to the antique air.

Comfortable Hotels

Albergo Duomo, Montepulciano

MAP F4 ▪ Via San Donato 14 ▪ 0578 757 473 ▪ www.albergoduomo montepulciano.it ▪ €

This family-run inn just steps from the Duomo adds rustic accents such as wooden dressers and iron bedsteads to the modern decor. There's a small courtyard for summer breakfasts.

AnticheMura, Arezzo

MAP F3 ▪ Piaggia di Murello 35 ▪ 3473 149 146 ▪ Wi-Fi ▪ www. antichemura.info ▪ €

The shell is old Tuscany but inside are six bright rooms individually decorated and named after women from history and the arts, including Baroque painter Artemisia Gentileschi and Audrey Hepburn's Holly Golightly. Breakfast is served in a room streetside.

Davanzati, Florence

MAP M4 ▪ Via Porta Rossa 5 ▪ 055 286 666 ▪ Wi-Fi ▪ www.hotel davanzati.it ▪ €€

Davanzati is set on a medieval street in the historic core of Florence. Rooms are decorated in traditional Tuscan style, with terracotta floors, including in several family rooms. The friendly hosts offer a daily free aperitif happy hour.

Dei Capitani, Montalcino

MAP E4 ▪ Via Lapini 6 ▪ 0577 847 227 ▪ Wi-Fi ▪ www.deicapitani.it ▪ €€

Located in the historic centre of town, this was once a barracks for the Sienese army in their last stand against Florentine forces. Now its rustic rooms exude comfort and serenity, with sweeping valley views from the rooms at the back and lofted mini-apartments on the street side. There's also a small terrace pool.

Hotel Pendini, Florence

MAP M3 ▪ Via Strozzi 2 ▪ 055 211 170 ▪ Wi-Fi ▪ www.hotelpendini.it ▪ €€

Little has changed here for over 120 years, save the addition of firm beds and new furnishings. The larger rooms overlooking Piazza della Repubblica are best. The Abbolafaio brothers' welcome is warm, and they have two other hotels in town (one near the station, the other on the Arno).

Hotel San Michele, Cortona

MAP F4 ▪ Via Guelfa 15 ▪ 0575 604 348 ▪ www. hotelsanmichele.net ▪ €

Hotel San Michele is a 15th-century palazzo of High Renaissance architectural panache, with creamy plaster against soft grey stone. The hotel features beamed ceilings, antiques and rural vistas from many rooms, and yet is sited right in the centre of town.

Hotel Scilla, Sovana

MAP F6 ▪ Via Rodolfo Siviero 3 ▪ 3491 245 540 ▪ www.albergo scilla.com ▪ €

In the centre of one of Tuscany's most charming villages, rooms spread over three buildings mix the contemporary and the antique – exposed walls and engraved headboards vie with modern baths and glass table tops. The on-site restaurant is good, and staff are friendly.

La Luna, Lucca

MAP C2 ▪ Via Filungo, Corte Compagni 12 ▪ 0583 493 634 ▪ www. hotellaluna.it ▪ €€

This family-run hotel is in a cul-de-sac off Lucca's main shopping street. The rooms are split between two buildings; most furnishings are modern, but try to get a second-floor room in the older half of the hotel, which retain some original 17th-century frescoes.

Patria, Pistoia

MAP D2 ▪ Via F Crispi 8 ▪ 0573 358 800 ▪ www. patriahotel.com ▪ €€

Pistoia has a dearth of decent hotels, but this Patria is a modern place. It has amenities such as baby- and dog-sitting services, and a great location between the train station and the Duomo.

Santa Caterina, Siena

MAP E4 ▪ Via Enea Silvio Picolomini 7 ▪ 0577 221 105 ▪ Wi-Fi ▪ www. hotelsantacaterina siena.com ▪ €€

There are plenty of oak and manor-house-style fittings in the rooms. Those facing south have unforgettable views over the hills south of Siena.

Budget Gems

Bernini, Siena

MAP E4 ▪ Via della Sapienza 15 ▪ 0577 289 047 ▪ www.albergo-bernini.com ▪ €

A tiny, family-run hotel, Bernini books up quickly.

The collection of white-washed rooms atop the convent of St Catherine are quiet. Some have views of the Duomo, several have air conditioning and a handful are en suite.

Il Colombaio, Castellina in Chianti

MAP E3 ▪ Via Chiantigiana 29 ▪ 0577 740 444 ▪ www. albergoilcolombaio.it ▪ €

A converted farmhouse, Il Colombaio has retained a strong country air, with rustic antiques and bucolic vistas. Large rooms open off cosy lounges. There's also a small pool.

Italia, Cortona

MAP F4 ▪ Via Ghibellina 5/7 ▪ 0575 630 254 ▪ www.hotelitalia cortona.com ▪ €

Just a few steps off the main piazza, the Italia offers standard comforts and modern furnishings. A few rooms have views of the countryside beyond Cortona's rooftops.

La Dimora del Corso, Montepulciano

MAP F4 ▪ Via di Gracciano nel Corso 33 ▪ 3662 649 441 ▪ Wi-Fi ▪ www.ladimoranelcorso. com/it ▪ €

Halfway up the main street, just steps from the 16th-century Torre di Pulcinella (a Neapolitan character analogous to the British Mr Punch) is this three-floored B&B. The rooms (some with terraces) have been renovated, with air conditioning and elevator access. The owners have another B&B, a restaurant and three apartments nearby.

Locanda del Vino Nobile, near Montepulciano

MAP F4 ▪ Via dei Lillà 1, Sant' Albino di Montepulciano ▪ 0578 321 1498 ▪ Wi-Fi ▪ €

This B&B offers five rooms with terracotta tiles and wooden ceilings, set above an excellent Tuscan restaurant. Breakfast is an event, with fresh fruit and home-baked cakes. The roadside location is ideal for those touring the countryside by car.

Locanda Orchidea, Florence

MAP P3 ▪ Borgo degli Albizi 11 ▪ 3335 222 295 ▪ Wi-Fi ▪ www.locanda orchidea.it ▪ €

Simply decorated rooms with cool tiled floors and private bathrooms are tucked away in the shuttered 13th-century Palazzo Donati, whose façade was designed by Buontalenti. It is thought that Dante's wife, Gemma Donati, was born here. The rooms at the back overlook a quiet, leafy courtyard. The English owner is a good source of information about the city.

Piccolo Hotel Etruria, Siena

MAP E4 ▪ Via delle Donzelle 3 ▪ 0577 288 088 ▪ www.hoteletruria. com ▪ €

In a centre plagued by either overpriced or grotty hotels, tiny Etruria stands proud. In a 16th-century building close to Piazza del Campo, its basic rooms with contemporary decor are great value and very popular. The only drawback is the 1am curfew. Book early.

For a key to hotel price categories see p142

Piccolo Hotel Puccini, Lucca

MAP C2 ▪ Via di Poggio 9 ▪ 058 355 421 ▪ www. hotelpuccini.com ▪ €
In this hotel, all but two of the smallish but nicely furnished rooms are on the front. If you lean out, you can see the Romanesque façade of San Michele.

Porta Castellana, Montalcino

MAP E4 ▪ Via Santa Lucia 20 ▪ 0577 839 001 ▪ Wi-Fi ▪ www.portacastellana. com ▪ €
This B&B has been crafted out of a former storehouse with barrel-vaulted ceilings and designed with a keen eye and good taste. Breakfast is brought to your room or served in a garden with views over the Val d'Orcia.

Vizi Ottavo, Castiglion Fiorentino

MAP F4 ▪ Via San Michele 69 ▪ 0575 657 319 ▪ Wi-Fi ▪ www.viziottavo. com ▪ €
The "eighth vice" B&B has bold-coloured rooms with chromatherapy showers, each styled after one of the seven deadly sins. Second-floor Ira (Anger) and Invidia (Envy) have terraces. The honeymoon suite (Lust, of course) has great views.

Agriturismi

Fattoria Castello di Pratelli, Incisa

MAP E3 ▪ Via di Pratelli 1A ▪ 0558 335 986 ▪ Closed Nov & Dec ▪ Wi-Fi ▪ www. castellodipratelli.it ▪ €
A turretted fortress from the Dark Ages with eight spacious apartments anchors this wine and olive oil estate. There's also a pool, and mountain bikes

for hire. The minimum stay is three nights on weekends in low season.

Fattoria Castello di Verrazzano, Greve in Chianti

MAP E3 ▪ Via Castello di Verrazzano 1 ▪ 055 854 243 ▪ www.verrazzano. com ▪ €
A 12th-century castle and wine estate offering cosy rooms and spacious apartments (weekly). Cantina visits and wine tastings available, and the restaurant is good.

Il Cicalino, Massa Marittima

MAP D4/5 ▪ Loc Cicalino ▪ 0566 902 031 ▪ www. ilcicalino.it ▪ €€
This complex of converted buildings in a farm/park offers flats to let as a whole or by room. The property has a Tuscan restaurant, pool, football pitch and gym. Mountain-bike rental is available.

Podere Marcampo, near Volterra

MAP D4 ▪ Loc S Cipriano 30 ▪ 058 885 393 ▪ Wi-Fi ▪ www.poderemarcampo. com ▪ €
Modern-rustic rooms and apartments in a farmhouse with an outdoor pool and stunning views back to Volterra. The estate's own wines are excellent. Half board is available at Volterra's Del Duca restaurant (see p119), which is owned by the same family.

Podere Terreno, Radda in Chianti

MAP E3 ▪ Localita' Volpaia ▪ 0577 057 719, 3477 953 620 ▪ www. podereterreno.it ▪ €€
The welcome is warm at this old, family-run

countryside smallholding of rustic rooms with original features. Unlike most *agriturismi*, you dine with the hosts and other guests at a long table.

Tenuta Castello il Corno, San Casciano

MAP E3 ▪ Via Malafrasca 64 ▪ 055 824 851 ▪ Closed Jan & Feb ▪ Wi-Fi ▪ www.tenutailcorno.com ▪ €€
Apartments and rooms are available in former peasant quarters around a fine vineyard villa. You can also learn Tuscan cooking.

Fattoria Maionchi, Lucca

MAP C2 ▪ Loc Tofori ▪ 0583 978 194 ▪ www. fattoriamaionchi.it ▪ €€
The four large, multilevel apartments, sleeping four to six, are country-styled and set in pretty gardens. The minimum stay is three nights in low season.

Grazia, Orbetello

MAP E6 ▪ Via Aurelia 4/b ▪ 0564 881 182 ▪ www. agriturismograzia.com ▪ €€
This 18th-century villa is surrounded by apartments that sleep two to four people. Bicycles are free for guests and are equipped with child seats and the nature reserves are close by.

I Bonsi, Reggello

MAP E3 ▪ Via I Bonsi 47, Loc Sant'Agata ▪ 0558 652 118 ▪ www.agri turismoibonsi.it ▪ €€€
A tree-lined avenue leads to this magnif-icent country residence set in parkland over-looking the Arno valley.

There are rustic apartments to let. Two-night minimum stay.

Villa Vignamaggio, Greve in Chianti

MAP E3 ■ Via Petriolo 5 ■ 055 854 661 ■ www.vignamaggio.com ■ €€€

The birthplace of Mona Lisa, this 14th-century villa (see p64) and its surrounding cottages make a sumptuous *agriturismo* (see p40). The rooms are painted in strong colours, and the gardens were featured in the film *Much Ado About Nothing*. Tennis courts and two pools round it off. The apartments have Jacuzzis and cooking facilities. Minimum stay is two nights.

Countryside Hotel Retreats

Villa La Principessa, near Lucca

MAP C2 ■ Via Nuova per Pisa 1616/G, Loc Massa Pisana ■ 0583 370 963 ■ Wi-Fi ■ www.hotelprincipessalucca.it ■ €€

This was once the court of the 12th-century Duke of Lucca. The rooms are large and comfortable, and there is a swimming pool and garden.

Villa Rosa in Boscorotondo, Panzano

MAP E3 ■ Strada Provinciale 2bis 65 ■ 3517 087 800 ■ www.resortvillarosa.it ■ €

This isolated villa stands on a forested stretch of Chianti roadside. The spacious rooms feature beamed ceilings. Two large terraces are accessible through the front rooms. There's a

pool, woodland trails and set dinners on the terrace in summer.

Casa Campanella, Elba

MAP C5 ■ Piano di Mola ■ 0565 915 740 ■ Closed Nov–Mar ■ Wi-Fi ■ www.casacampanella.it ■ €€

Stay in mini-apartments in large grounds wth an outdoor pool amid the quiet of the Elban countryside. Capoliveri's nightlife and the beaches at Zuccale and Barabarca are within 1.5 km (1 mile).

Castello di Gargonza, Monte San Savino

MAP F4 ■ Loc Gargonza ■ 0575 847 021 ■ Wi-Fi ■ www.gargonza.it ■ €€

This medieval castle turned spectacular hostelry is set in a charming 13th-century fortified village. Although far from civilization, the Castello di Gargonza, with its fine restaurant, and a pool just outside the village walls, feels less removed than many a rural retreat. Both rooms and self-catering apartments are available.

Castello Ripa d'Orcia, San Quirico d'Orcia

MAP F4 ■ Loc Ripa d'Orcia ■ 0577 897 376 ■ www.castelloripadorcia.com ■ €€

A fairy-tale hotel hewn from a 13th-century castle and outbuildings immersed in the green hills of a nature reserve. Relaxation is the order of your stay, with an absence of TVs and telephones in the huge, country-styled rooms and apartments.

Relais San Pietro, Castiglion Fiorentino

MAP F4 ■ Loc Polvano 3 ■ 0575 650 100 ■ Closed Nov–Apr ■ Wi-Fi ■ €€

A 17th-century farmhouse, this is in an idyllic location overlooking a valley. Guests can choose to stay in the main building or a converted priest's house. Dinner is often served on the terrace in summer.

Castello di Spaltenna, Gaiole

MAP E3 ■ Pieve di Spaltenna ■ 0577 749 483 ■ Wi-Fi ■ www.spaltenna.it ■ €€

Around the core of a 12th-century castle, this is the Chianti's most luxurious inn. It has a room for wine tasting, an outdoor pool and a plethora of antiques. Corner rooms, with their ceiling beams, are best.

Locanda dell' Amorosa, Sinalunga

MAP F4 ■ Loc L'Amorosa ■ 0577 677 211 ■ Wi-Fi ■ www.amorosa.it ■ €€€

The "Lover's Inn" moniker dates back to the hotel's 14th-century origins. The apartment-like accommodation has a refined rustic style under the more formal brick loggias around the courtyard.

Il Borro Relais & Chateaux, Il Borro

MAP F3 ■ Loc Il Borro 1 ■ 055 977 053 ■ www.ilborro.it ■ €€€

This hamlet dating back to Roman times was bought in 1993 and restored by the Ferragamo family. Il Borro features varying accommodation including suites in the ancient village. Yoga, golf, cookery classes, craft workshops and wine tours are also offered.

For a key to hotel price categories see p142

Villa La Massa, Candeli

MAP E3 ▪ Via della Massa 24 ▪ 055 62 611 ▪ Closed Nov–Mar ▪ www.villa lamassa.com ▪ €€€

Everyone from Churchill to Madonna has stayed in this Renaissance villa turned hotel. Tennis courts, a pool and a Tuscan restaurant overlooking the Arno justify its prestigious reputation.

Hotels with a View

Hotel Duomo, Siena

MAP E4 ▪ Via Stalloreggi 38 ▪ 0577 289 088 ▪ www. hotelduomo.it ▪ €

Even though the palazzo is from the 12th century, the rooms – some medium-sized, others a bit small – are modern and comfortable. The 12 "panoramic" rooms that feature Duomo views include a small top-floor double room with windows on three sides and sweeping vistas of Siena.

La Cisterna, San Gimignano

MAP D3 ▪ Piazza Cisterna 23 ▪ 0577 940 328 ▪ www. hotelcisterna.it ▪ €

You can pick your views at this hotel – front rooms have a view of the piazza and the town's famous towers, the back rooms look over vineyards and hills. A cinematographers' favourite, the hotel put in an appearance in *Tea with Mussolini* and *Where Angels Fear to Tread*.

Le Cetinelle, near Greve in Chianti

MAP E3 ▪ Via Canonica 13 ▪ 0558 544 745 ▪ Wi-Fi ▪ www.cetinelle.com ▪ €

Watch the sky turn pink as a hazy sun sinks into the hills above Greve from this isolated farmhouse B&B with an outdoor pool. Individually themed Tuscan rooms do the spectacular setting justice.

Montorio, Montepulciano

MAP F4 ▪ Strada per Pienza 2 ▪ 0578 717 442 ▪ Closed Dec–Feb ▪ Wi-Fi ▪ www.montorio.com ▪ €

This small hilltop hotel consists of comfortable mini-apartments. The garden has the best views of the Tempio di San Biagio; all rooms have rural vistas. Minimum stay three nights.

Antica Dimora Johlea, Florence

MAP E3 ▪ Via San Gallo 80 ▪ 0554 633 292 ▪ Wi-Fi ▪ €€

No Florence hotel in this price bracket has such a spectacular terrace, looking across the tiled rooftops to Brunelleschi's dome. The interiors are decked out like a stylish Florentine home (or *dimora*), with parquet floors, dark wood and busy patterns.

Hotel Bigallo, Florence

MAP M3 ▪ Vicolo degli Adimari 2 ▪ 055 216 086 ▪ www.hotelbigallo florence.com ▪ €€

Located in the very heart of Florence's historic core, near the Duomo, the family-run Bigallo has long been famous among budget-conscious travellers for its views of the magnificent cathedral group. The only drawback here is the noise of passing pedestrians.

Il Giglio, Montalcino

MAP E4 ▪ Via Soccorso Saloni 5 ▪ 0577 848 167 ▪ www.giglio hotel.com ▪ €€

Only the eight rooms at the back enjoy the best view in town – a slope down to Tuscany's countryside on one side and cliff-hugging houses on the other. This hotel adds a touch of class to the rustic ambience.

Torre Guelfa, Florence

MAP M4 ▪ Borgo SS Apostoli 8 ▪ 0552 396 338 ▪ www. hoteltorreguelfa.com ▪ €€

While most rooms in this converted 1280 palazzo don't have great views, the lofty terrace bar has an unbeatable panorama across Florence.

Villa Kinzica, Pisa

MAP C3 ▪ Piazza Arcivescovado 2 ▪ 050 560 419 ▪ www.hotel villakinzica.com ▪ €€

Although the hotel is nothing special, if you get a room on the front or left side you will open your shutters on a postcard view of the Leaning Tower.

Torre di Bellosguardo, Florence

MAP E3 ▪ Via Roti Michelozzi 2 ▪ 0552 298 145 ▪ www.torrebellos guardo.com ▪ €€€

The views from Fiesole are famous, but the panorama from Bellosguardo hill above the Oltrarno is better – a close-up sweep of the Florence skyline from the gardens and pool of an evocatively medieval retreat. The central tower contains a suite which features unsurpassed views in all four directions.

Monasteries and Youth Hostels

Abbazia di Monte Oliveto Maggiore

MAP E4 ▪ Abbazia di Monte Oliveto Maggiore ▪ 0577 707 611 ▪ Closed Nov ▪ No credit cards ▪ www.monteoliveto maggiore.it ▪ €

This gorgeously frescoed monastery in the hills offers single and double rooms with private baths, and also sells honey, herbs and wines. The drive to the monastery is a Tuscan classic.

Camping Village Torre Pendente, Pisa

MAP C3 ▪ Viale delle Cascine 86 ▪ 050 561 704 ▪ Closed Nov-Mar ▪ Wi-Fi ▪ www.camping torrependente.it ▪ €

Only 800 metres (half-a-mile) from the Leaning Tower, the property offers mobile home rooms and camping pitches with free showers. There's a mini market, a café, barbecue pits, a pool and a pizzeria.

Foresteria Volterra, Volterra

MAP D4 ▪ Loc San Girolamo ▪ 058 880 050 ▪ Wi-Fi ▪ www.foresteria volterra.it ▪ €

This purpose-built hostel, located in the woods just outside the eastern gates of Volterra, has spacious modern rooms, from singles up to quads. The rooms are all private and

have en suite bathrooms and a small private outdoor terrace.

Ostello Bello Firenze

MAP M2 ▪ Via Faenza 56 ▪ 055 213 806 ▪ www. ostellobello.com/en/ hostel/florence ▪ €

Situated in the San Lorenzo neighbourhood, this hotel offers all the comforts of home, including complimentary toiletries, work stations for digital nomads, board games and musical instruments. Every room – from a private single room to a larger dormitory – has an en suite toilet.

Lucca Charm

MAP C2 ▪ Via Roma 14 ▪ 3929 326 838 ▪ www. affittacamere-lucca.it ▪ €

Featuring traditional Lucchese-style interiors, this B&B is located in the city's historic centre. It has four clean rooms with en suite facilities. Breakfast is served in a nearby bar.

Ostello Archi Rossi, Florence

MAP M2 ▪ Via Faenza 94r ▪ 055 290 804 ▪ Wi-Fi ▪ www.hostelarchirossi. com ▪ €

This popular, well-located hostel caters to families, individuals and groups. It has good facilities, but not all rooms are en suite.

Ostello del Chianti, Tavernelle Val di Pesa

MAP E3 ▪ Via Roma 137 ▪ 0558 050 265 ▪ www. ostellodelchianti.it ▪ €

The activities here are geared toward wine production and tasting. It has a few family rooms. Breakfast and packed lunch is available at an extra cost. SITA buses stop nearby.

Plus Florence, Florence

MAP E3 ▪ Via Santa Caterina d'Alessandria 15 ▪ 0556 286 347 ▪ Wi-Fi ▪ www.plushostels.com ▪ €€

This hostel has better facilities than most pricey city hotels, including an outdoor pool (summer), an indoor pool and a Turkish bath (winter only). Private rooms in the new building have the best furnishings. All rooms are en suite.

Santuario Santa Caterina/Alma Domus, Siena

MAP E4 ▪ Via Camporeggio 37 ▪ 057 744 177 ▪ www.hotel almadomus.it ▪ €

The nuns of St Catherine run this simple but comfortable inn. Many of the rooms have great views across a narrow valley to the striped Duomo. All the rooms have air conditioning. There's a television lounge and pay phones in the common rooms.

Suore Oblate dell'Assunzione, Florence

MAP P3 ▪ Borgo Pinti 15 ▪ 0552 346 291 ▪ Wi-Fi ▪ www.oblate.it/en ▪ €

A Medici-era palace, this is now run by nuns as a peaceful guesthouse. The rooms are basic but comfortable and spacious, and the sisters are very welcoming. It is also right in the centre: almost everything major in the city is within walking distance from the front door. There is a minimum stay of two nights.

For a key to hotel price categories see p142

General Index

Acknowledgments

This edition updated by
Contributor Toni DeBella
Senior Editor Alison McGill
Senior Designers Laura O'Brien,
Vinita Venugopal
Project Editors Dipika Dasgupta, Alex Pathe
Project Art Editor Ankita Sharma
Assistant Editor Tavleen Kaur
Picture Research Administrator Vagisha Pushp
Picture Research Manager Taiyaba Khatoon
Publishing Assistant Halima Mohammed
Jacket Designer Jordan Lambley
Cartographer Ashif
Cartography Manager Suresh Kumar
Senior DTP Designer Tanveer Zaidi
Senior Production Editor Jason Little
Senior Production Controller Samantha Cross
Deputy Editorial Manager Beverly Smart
Managing Editors Shikha Kulkarni,
Hollie Teague
Managing Art Editor Sarah Snelling
Senior Managing Art Editor Priyanka Thakur
Art Director Maxine Pedliham
Publishing Director Georgina Dee

DK would like to thank the following for their contribution to the previous editions: Hilary Bird, Reid Bramblett, Samantha Cook, Federico Damonte, Donald Strachan

Dagli Orti 20tl, /G. Nimatallah 12cla, 20cb, S. Vannini 56bc; DEA Picture Library 13tl, 37tl, 55b; EyeEm /Simon Marlow 10clb; Lonely Planet Images /Richard I'Anson 99tl; Mondadori Portfolio 32cb, 43br; Friedrich Schmidt 91bl; Visions of Our Land 83tl.

iStockphoto.com: sborisov 100-1.

La Bottega del Rame: 124cb.

La Botteghina del Ceramista: Giovanni Todesca 85cb.

Ora d'Aria: 87tl.

IO Osteria Personale: 87cr.

Ristorante Enoteca "Del Duca": 119cr.

Robert Harding Picture Library: Yoko Aziz 38clb, Markus Lange 2tr, 48-9.

Romano Vireggio: 113tl.

Photo Scala, Florence: Mario Bonotto 18cla, 36clb, 57tr; Photo Opera Metropolitana Siena 14bc, 15ca, 51br, 58b, 55c.

SuperStock: Universal Images Group/ Photoservice Electa 52tr.

Cover
Front and spine: **123RF.com:** Leandro Henrich.

Back: **Alamy Stock Photo:** Konrad Wothe cla; **Dreamstime.com:** Adisa crb, Minnystock tl, Ariadna De Raadt tr; **123RF.com:** Leandro Henrich b.

Pull Out Map Cover
123RF.com: Leandro Henrich.

All other images © Dorling Kindersley
For further information see: www.dkimages.com

Illustrator Chris Orr & Associates

First edition 2002

First published in Great Britain by Dorling Kindersley Limited DK, One Embassy Gardens, 8 Viaduct Gardens, London SW11 7BW, UK

The authorised representative in the EEA is Dorling Kindersley Verlag GmbH. Arnulfstr. 124, 80636 Munich, Germany

Published in the United States by DK Publishing, 1745 Broadway, 20th Floor, New York, NY 10019, USA

Copyright © 2002, 2023 Dorling Kindersley Limited

A Penguin Random House Company

23 24 25 26 10 9 8 7 6 5 4 3 2 1

A CIP catalogue record is available from the British Library.

A catalogue record for this book is available from the Library of Congress.

ISSN 1479-344X
ISBN 978-0-2416-1872-1

Printed and bound in Malaysia

www.dk.com

As a guide to abbreviations in visitor information blocks: **Adm** = admission charge; **L** = lunch; **D** = dinner.

MIX
Paper | Supporting responsible forestry
FSC™ C018179

This book was made with Forest Stewardship Council™ certified paper – one small step in DK's commitment to a sustainable future.
For more information go to www.dk.com/our-green-pledge